Django and JavaScript

Building Scalable Full-Stack Applications with Python, React, and Vue.js

Thompson Carter

Rafael Sanders

Miguel Farmer

Contents

Introduction – Navigating Full-Stack Development 14

Overview of Full-Stack Development 14

The Front-End (Client-Side) 16

The Back-End (Server-Side) 18

Why Choose Django with React and Vue.js? ... 19

Django: Powering the Back-End 20

React: Building Interactive Front-Ends 23

Vue.js: A Simplified Alternative to React 25

How Django, React, and Vue.js Complement Each Other 27

Who This Book is For 28

Conclusion: The Road Ahead 30

Chapter 1: Introduction to Django (Backend) 32

What is Django? 32

1. Batteries-Included Philosophy 34

2. Security 34

3. Scalability 35

4. Robust Database Handling 35

5. Developer-Friendly......................................35

6. Versatility..36

Setting Up Django 36

Step 1: Installing Python..............................37

Step 2: Setting Up a Virtual Environment...............38

Step 3: Installing Django..............................40

Step 4: Creating a New Django Project 41

Step 5: Running the Development Server................42

Creating a Basic Django Project: A Hands-On

CRUD Application...43

Step 1: Creating a Django App 44

Step 2: Defining the Model..............................45

Step 3: Registering the Model with the Admin Site..46

Step 4: Creating the Views..............................47

Step 5: Creating the Forms..............................50

Step 6: Creating the Templates............................50

Step 7: URL Routing.....................................53

Conclusion 55

Chapter 2: Introduction to React (Frontend)..56

What is React? 56

Component-Based Architecture 58

Declarative Syntax 58

Virtual DOM 59

Unidirectional Data Flow 60

Why Use React? 60

Setting Up React 62

Step 1: Install Node.js 63

Step 2: Install Create React App 64

Step 3: Create a New React Project 64

Step 4: Start the Development Server 65

Building Your First React Component 66

Step 1: Creating a New Component 67

Step 2: Explaining the Code 69

Step 3: Rendering the Component 70

Step 4: Testing the Component 71

Conclusion 72

Chapter 3: Introduction to Vue.js (Frontend) . 74

What is Vue.js? 75

Vue vs. React: A Quick Comparison 77

Setting Up Vue.js 79

Step 1: Install Node.js and npm 80

Step 2: Install Vue CLI 81

Step 3: Create a New Vue Project 82

Step 4: Run the Development Server 83

Creating Your First Vue Component 84

Step 1: Create a Vue Component 84

Step 2: Breaking Down the Code 87

Step 3: Use the Component in the App 89

Step 4: Testing the Application 90

Conclusion 91

Chapter 4: Building the Backend with Django 93

Building Models, Views, and Templates 94

1. Models: Defining the Data Structure 95

.... 99

2. Views: Handling Logic and Displaying Content ... 99

3. Templates: Rendering HTML Views 103

Django REST Framework (DRF) 108

1. Installing Django REST Framework 109

2. Creating Serializers 110

3. Creating API Views 111

4. Setting Up URLs for the API 112

Conclusion 113

Chapter 5: Connecting Django with React.... 115

Fetching Data with React 116

Step 1: Setting Up Django API Endpoints.............. 117

Step 2: Setting Up React for Data Fetching........... 120

Step 3: Displaying the TaskList Component in the
App 124

State Management with React 125

1. Understanding React State 126

2. Using useState for Local State..................... 127

3. Managing More Complex Data with State 128

4. Using Context API for Global State Management
.... 130

5. Advanced State Management with Redux........... 134

Conclusion 134

Chapter 6: Connecting Django with Vue.js ... 136

Vue.js Components and Data Binding........... 137

1. Setting Up Vue.js 138

2. Creating Vue Components.................................... 140

3. Vue.js Data Binding.. 147

Vue Router for Navigation............................. 151

1. Installing Vue Router.. 152

2. Setting Up Vue Router 153

Conclusion 159

Chapter 7: Authentication and Authorization

.... 161

User Authentication with Django.................... 162

1. Setting Up Authentication in Django 163

2. Using Third-Party Authentication Tools............. 170

Securing the React/Vue Frontend.................... 173

1. Securing Authentication with JWT 174

Conclusion 185

Chapter 8: Optimizing the Full-Stack Application

.... 187

Performance Tuning with Django................... 188

1. Caching in Django 189

2. Database Indexing 193

3. Query Optimization 196

Optimizing React/Vue.js 198

1. Optimizing React Performance 199

2. Optimizing Vue.js Performance 204

Conclusion 208

Chapter 9: Building a Blog Application........ 210

Setting Up the Backend: Django.................... 211

1. Setting Up Django Project........................... 212

2. Setting Up Views and URLs 217

Building the Frontend: React...................... 224

1. Setting Up React 224

2. Displaying Blog Posts 225

3. Adding Post Editing................................. 231

Conclusion 235

**Chapter 10: Building an E-Commerce
Application 237**

Setting Up the Backend: Django.................... 238

1. Setting Up Django Project........................... 239

2. Creating Models for Products and Orders.......... 241

3. Setting Up Product and Cart Views 245

4. Handling Payments with Stripe 250

Building the Frontend: React or Vue.js 253

1. Setting Up React 254

2. Setting Up Vue.js 257

Conclusion 260

Conclusion: Next Steps in Full-Stack Development 262

Scaling Your Application 263

1. Load Balancing 264

2. Horizontal Scaling 267

3. Vertical Scaling 269

4. Microservices Architecture 271

Learning Resources and Continuing Education

.... 273

1. Books to Deepen Your Knowledge 274

2. Online Courses 275

3. Blogs and Online Communities 277

4. Developer Conferences and Meetups 279

Conclusion 280

[11]

Appendices **282**

Appendix A: Common Errors and

Troubleshooting 282

    1. Django Errors 283

    2. React Errors 287

    3. Vue.js Errors 292

Appendix B: Recommended Tools and

Libraries 296

    1. Django Tools and Libraries 297

    2. React Tools and Libraries 299

    3. Vue.js Tools and Libraries 301

    Conclusion 303

How to Scan a Barcode to Get a Repository

1. **Install a QR/Barcode Scanner** – Ensure you have a barcode or QR code scanner app installed on your smartphone or use a built-in scanner in **GitHub, GitLab, or Bitbucket.**

2. **Open the Scanner** – Launch the scanner app and grant necessary camera permissions.

3. **Scan the Barcode** – Align the barcode within the scanning frame. The scanner will automatically detect and process it.

4. **Follow the Link** – The scanned result will display a **URL to the repository**. Tap the link to open it in your web browser or Git client.

5. **Clone the Repository** – Use **Git clone** with the provided URL to download the repository to your local machine.

[13]

Introduction – Navigating Full-Stack Development

In the world of web development, understanding how different technologies work together to build dynamic, scalable applications is essential. Full-stack development is at the heart of this understanding, combining both the front-end and back-end to deliver seamless user experiences. In this chapter, we will explore the concept of full-stack development, delve into the roles of front-end and back-end technologies, and discuss why Django with React and Vue.js are powerful tools for modern web development.

Overview of Full-Stack Development

Full-stack development refers to the practice of working with both the front-end (client-side) and the back-end (server-side) parts of a web application. A full-stack developer is someone who can develop both the user-facing part of an application and the server-side logic that powers it.

In simpler terms, full-stack developers are like Swiss Army knives—they can handle the entire web development process. They write code for the visible parts of an app that users interact with (front-end) and also write the behind-the-scenes code that manages data, user authentication, and application logic (back-end).

The Front-End (Client-Side)

The front-end of an application is everything that users see and interact with directly in their browser. It's the "user interface" (UI) of a website or application, and it's built with HTML, CSS, and JavaScript. These technologies allow developers to design and structure content, style it to look visually appealing, and make it interactive.

Here are the primary components of front-end development:

- **HTML (HyperText Markup Language):** The skeleton of a web page, defining its structure with elements like headings, paragraphs, and links.

- **CSS (Cascading Style Sheets):** The style sheet that controls how HTML elements are displayed, from colors and fonts to layouts and animations.

- **JavaScript:** The programming language that brings web pages to life, enabling interactivity such as form validation, dynamic content loading, and animation.

The Back-End (Server-Side)

The back-end refers to the server-side of a web application. It's the behind-the-scenes code that manages data, business logic, user authentication, and application flow. This part of the stack is responsible for receiving requests from the front-end, processing them, and returning appropriate data or responses.

Back-end technologies typically involve:

- **Databases:** Where data is stored, such as MySQL, PostgreSQL, or MongoDB. These systems allow the back-end to store, retrieve, and manipulate data.

- **Server-Side Languages:** Languages like Python, Java, Ruby, or Node.js are used to write the logic that powers a website.

- **Frameworks:** These are collections of libraries and tools that help developers build web applications more efficiently. For instance, Django is a Python-based framework, while Node.js is often paired with Express.

Why Choose Django with React and Vue.js?

Now that we've introduced the concept of full-stack development, let's dive into why Django, React, and Vue.js are the go-to technologies for modern, scalable applications. Each of these frameworks is popular in the industry for different reasons, but together they offer a powerful combination for building web applications that are not only functional but also user-friendly and maintainable.

Django: Powering the Back-End

What is Django?

Django is a high-level Python web framework that simplifies the development of web applications by providing an organized structure, reusable components, and tools to handle common tasks. It's designed to help developers build secure and scalable applications quickly, without reinventing the wheel. Django is known for its "batteries-included" approach, meaning it provides a wide range of features out of the box.

Key Strengths of Django:

- **Rapid Development:** Django includes many built-in tools for common tasks like authentication, form handling, and URL routing, allowing developers to focus on building unique features instead of writing repetitive code.

- **Security:** Django is secure by default. It provides robust protection against common security threats like SQL injection, cross-site scripting (XSS), and cross-site request forgery (CSRF).

- **Scalability:** Django's architecture is designed for scalability, making it suitable for projects of all sizes—from small personal blogs to large-scale, high-traffic websites.

Example Project with Django: Imagine you're building a simple task management app where users can create and manage tasks. With Django, you could quickly set up models for tasks, user authentication, and views that display tasks in a dynamic way. Django's ORM (Object-Relational Mapping) system makes it easy to interact with your database without writing SQL queries.

React: Building Interactive Front-Ends

What is React?

React is a JavaScript library for building user interfaces, particularly single-page applications (SPAs). Developed and maintained by Facebook, React is designed to make it easy for developers to create dynamic, high-performance web applications with a smooth user experience.

Key Strengths of React:

- **Component-Based Architecture:** React allows developers to break down the user interface into smaller, reusable components. This modular approach makes the code more maintainable and easier to understand.

- **Virtual DOM:** React uses a virtual DOM to improve performance. Instead of updating the entire DOM when the state of an application changes, React only updates the parts of the DOM that need to change, making the app feel faster and more responsive.

- **Large Ecosystem and Community:** React has a huge community and ecosystem of third-party libraries, tools, and resources, making it easier for developers to find solutions to problems.

Example Project with React: Let's say you want to display a list of tasks fetched from your Django backend. With React, you would create a component to handle the display and interactivity of this list. React makes it easy to update the UI when a task is added or removed, providing a smooth, dynamic experience for users.

Vue.js: A Simplified Alternative to React

What is Vue.js?
Vue.js is a progressive JavaScript framework for building user interfaces. While React focuses on being a library for creating UIs, Vue.js is more of a full-fledged framework, offering features like state management, routing, and built-in components.

Key Strengths of Vue.js:

- **Simplicity and Flexibility:** Vue.js is known for its ease of integration with other projects and its gentle learning curve. It allows developers to incrementally adopt the framework, starting with just the view layer and scaling up as needed.

- **Two-Way Data Binding:** Vue.js offers two-way data binding, which means that any changes to the model (data) automatically update the view (UI), and vice versa. This makes it easier to handle user input and update the display dynamically.

- **Ecosystem and Tools:** Like React, Vue has an extensive ecosystem of libraries and tools that allow developers to extend its functionality to fit their needs.

Example Project with Vue.js: In a similar task management app, Vue.js would allow you to easily bind the tasks in your UI to the model (data) from the Django backend. With Vue's simplicity and reactivity, managing state and handling dynamic changes like adding or deleting tasks becomes straightforward.

How Django, React, and Vue.js Complement Each Other

Django, React, and Vue.js are all powerful in their own right, but when combined, they create a full-stack solution that handles both the front-end and back-end seamlessly.

- **Django for Back-End Logic:** Django's robust back-end features, including its ability to handle databases, routing, and user authentication, are perfect for managing the data that powers your application.

- **React/Vue.js for Front-End:** While Django handles the back-end, React and Vue.js bring the data to life on the front-end. React is ideal for building dynamic, high-performance interfaces, while Vue.js offers a simpler, more flexible solution with a focus on ease of use.

- **APIs as the Bridge:** Django's REST framework can be used to create APIs that connect the front-end and back-end. This allows React or Vue.js to fetch data from Django and update the UI dynamically.

By using Django with React or Vue.js, you get the best of both worlds: a powerful back-end that manages data and security, and a front-end that delivers smooth, dynamic user experiences.

Who This Book is For

This book is for anyone interested in learning full-stack development, whether you're a beginner just starting with Python and JavaScript or a professional looking to expand your skillset. Whether you're a hobbyist, freelancer, or developer working on client projects, the combination of Django, React, and Vue.js will equip you with the tools to build robust, scalable, and user-friendly web applications.

If you're someone who wants to learn how to:

- Build interactive web applications with Python and JavaScript

- Understand how the back-end and front-end work together

- Create scalable, dynamic web apps that users love to interact with

Then this book is for you.

By the end of this guide, you'll not only understand the theory behind full-stack development but also gain hands-on experience with building real-world applications. Each chapter will include practical projects that you can apply directly to your work or personal projects, giving you the confidence to take on full-stack challenges head-on.

Conclusion: The Road Ahead

Full-stack development is an exciting and rewarding journey that allows you to build complete applications, from the ground up. By combining Django with React or Vue.js, you are choosing to work with powerful technologies that will help you stay ahead in the world of web development. This book will guide you through the entire process, from learning the basics to building complex applications, ensuring that you understand both the theoretical and practical aspects of full-stack development.

So, let's dive into the exciting world of full-stack development, and start building the web applications of tomorrow!

Chapter 1: Introduction to Django (Backend)

Django is one of the most popular web frameworks used in the world today for building robust, scalable, and secure web applications. In this chapter, we'll explore what Django is, why it's such a strong choice for backend development, and how to set it up for the first time. We'll also walk through a hands-on project where you'll build a basic CRUD (Create, Read, Update, Delete) application to get familiar with Django's structure.

What is Django?

At its core, **Django** is a high-level Python web framework that simplifies the development of web applications. It was designed to help developers create complex, database-driven websites with minimal effort. The framework emphasizes rapid development, clean and pragmatic design, and scalability.

To understand why Django is so popular, let's look at some of its **core features**:

1. Batteries-Included Philosophy

One of Django's standout features is its "batteries-included" philosophy. This means that Django comes with a set of built-in features that make it easy for developers to get started quickly without having to worry about writing too much boilerplate code. Features such as user authentication, URL routing, database management, form handling, and more are included out-of-the-box.

2. Security

Django takes security seriously. It automatically provides protection against some of the most common security threats, such as SQL injection, cross-site scripting (XSS), cross-site request forgery (CSRF), and clickjacking. This means that, as a Django developer, you don't have to worry about implementing these complex security features manually.

3. Scalability

Django is built to scale. Whether you're working on a small personal project or a high-traffic web application, Django's design allows you to scale up your application without much hassle. Its modular architecture and efficient use of databases make it well-suited for larger applications.

4. Robust Database Handling

Django comes with its own **Object-Relational Mapping (ORM)** system, which allows you to interact with databases without writing SQL queries. The ORM maps database tables to Python classes, making database manipulation intuitive and easy to understand.

5. Developer-Friendly

Django emphasizes the importance of making life easier for developers. It comes with a built-in administrative interface that automatically generates a dashboard for managing data models, users, and more. The built-in development server allows you to test your application locally before deploying it.

6. Versatility

Django can be used for all types of web applications, including content management systems (CMS), social media platforms, scientific computing platforms, e-commerce sites, and more. It's also highly customizable, making it suitable for a wide range of use cases.

Setting Up Django

Before you start developing applications with Django, you need to set it up on your local machine. In this section, we'll walk through the steps to get Django running for the first time.

Step 1: Installing Python

Django is a Python framework, so you must have Python installed. If you haven't installed Python yet, follow these steps:

1. Download the latest version of Python from python.org.

2. Run the installer and follow the installation instructions. Be sure to check the box that says **"Add Python to PATH"** during installation.

3. Once installed, open your terminal or command prompt and type python --version to ensure Python is installed correctly.

Step 2: Setting Up a Virtual Environment

It's a good practice to set up a **virtual environment** for your Django projects. A virtual environment is an isolated environment where you can install packages (like Django) without affecting other projects on your machine.

Here's how to create and activate a virtual environment:

1. Open your terminal or command prompt and navigate to your project directory.

2. Run the following command to install virtualenv:

```
nginx
```

```
pip install virtualenv
```

3. Create a new virtual environment by running:

```
nginx
```

```
virtualenv venv
```

4. Activate the virtual environment:

  - On macOS/Linux:

```
bash
```

```
source venv/bin/activate
```

  - On Windows:

```
.\venv\Scripts\activate
```

5. Your terminal should now indicate that the virtual environment is active, usually with (venv) before your command prompt.

Step 3: Installing Django

Once your virtual environment is set up and active, you can install Django using pip, the Python package manager:

```
nginx
```

```
pip install django
```

To verify that Django was installed successfully, run the following command:

```
pgsql
```

```
django-admin --version
```

If you see the version number of Django, you're good to go!

Step 4: Creating a New Django Project

Now that Django is installed, you can create a new project. In your terminal, run the following command:

```
pgsql
```

```
django-admin startproject
myproject
```

This will create a new directory called myproject with the basic structure of a Django project. You should now have the following files and directories:

```
markdown
```

```
myproject/
    manage.py
    myproject/
        __init__.py
```

```
settings.py
urls.py
wsgi.py
```

- **manage.py**: A command-line utility for managing your project (like running the server, migrating the database, etc.).

- **settings.py**: The configuration file where you set up your database, security keys, and other settings.

- **urls.py**: Defines the URL routing for your application.

- **wsgi.py**: Used to deploy your application in a production environment.

Step 5: Running the Development Server

To ensure everything is working, run the development server using this command:

```
nginx
```

```
python manage.py runserver
```

You should see output like this:

```
nginx
```

```
Starting development server at
http://127.0.0.1:8000/
```

Open your browser and navigate to http://127.0.0.1:8000/. You should see the Django welcome page, confirming that the project is up and running.

Creating a Basic Django Project: A Hands-On CRUD Application

Now that Django is set up, it's time to dive into building your first application! In this project, we'll create a simple **CRUD** application. CRUD stands for **Create, Read, Update, and Delete —** the four basic operations you'll perform when working with data in web applications.

Step 1: Creating a Django App

A Django project can contain multiple apps. An app is a web component that does a specific task, like a blog, user authentication, or a product catalog.

Let's create an app called tasks:

```
nginx
```

```
python manage.py startapp tasks
```

This will create a directory called tasks with the following structure:

```
markdown
```

```
tasks/
    migrations/
        __init__.py
```

```
admin.py
apps.py
models.py
views.py
tests.py
urls.py
```

Step 2: Defining the Model

In Django, models define the structure of your database tables. We'll create a Task model with the following fields:

- title: A string to store the task title.

- description: A text field for the task description.

- completed: A boolean to track whether the task is completed or not.

In tasks/models.py, add the following code:

```
python
```

```python
from django.db import models


class Task(models.Model):
    title =
models.CharField(max_length=100)
    description =
models.TextField()
    completed =
models.BooleanField(default=False)

    def __str__(self):
        return self.title
```

Step 3: Registering the Model with the Admin Site

Django includes an automatic admin interface where you can manage your models. To make the Task model available in the admin site, open tasks/admin.py and add the following code:

```python
python
```

```
from django.contrib import admin
from .models import Task


admin.site.register(Task)
```

Step 4: Creating the Views

Views in Django are responsible for handling user requests and returning a response. We'll create views to handle displaying all tasks, adding a new task, updating a task, and deleting a task.

In tasks/views.py, add the following code:

```python
from django.shortcuts import
render, redirect
from .models import Task
from .forms import TaskForm

def task_list(request):
```

```
    tasks = Task.objects.all()
    return render(request,
'task_list.html', {'tasks':
tasks})

def task_add(request):
    if request.method == "POST":
        form =
TaskForm(request.POST)
        if form.is_valid():
            form.save()
            return
redirect('task_list')
    else:
        form = TaskForm()
    return render(request,
'task_form.html', {'form': form})

def task_update(request, pk):
    task = Task.objects.get(pk=pk)
    if request.method == "POST":
```

```python
        form =
TaskForm(request.POST,
instance=task)
        if form.is_valid():
            form.save()
            return
redirect('task_list')
    else:
        form =
TaskForm(instance=task)
    return render(request,
'task_form.html', {'form': form})

def task_delete(request, pk):
    task = Task.objects.get(pk=pk)
    task.delete()
    return redirect('task_list')
```

Step 5: Creating the Forms

Django provides a convenient way to handle forms. In this case, we'll use a form to manage the task data.

Create a new file tasks/forms.py and add the following code:

python

```python
from django import forms
from .models import Task

class TaskForm(forms.ModelForm):
    class Meta:
        model = Task
        fields = ['title',
'description', 'completed']
```

Step 6: Creating the Templates

Next, we'll create templates for displaying the task list and the form for adding or updating tasks.

Create a new directory tasks/templates and inside
it, create the following files:

- task_list.html

- task_form.html

For task_list.html, add the following code:

html

```
<!DOCTYPE html>
<html>
<head>
    <title>Task List</title>
</head>
<body>
    <h1>Task List</h1>
    <ul>
        {% for task in tasks %}
            <li>{{ task.title }} -
{% if task.completed %} Completed
```

```
{% else %} Pending {% endif
%}</li>
        {% endfor %}
    </ul>
    <a href="{% url 'task_add'
%}">Add New Task</a>
</body>
</html>
```

For task_form.html, add this:

html

```
<!DOCTYPE html>
<html>
<head>
    <title>Task Form</title>
</head>
<body>
    <h1>Task Form</h1>
    <form method="post">
        {% csrf_token %}
        {{ form.as_p }}
```

```
    <button
type="submit">Save</button>
    </form>
</body>
</html>
```

Step 7: URL Routing

The final step is to create URLs to map the views we just created. Open tasks/urls.py and add the following:

python

```python
from django.urls import path
from . import views

urlpatterns = [
    path('', views.task_list,
name='task_list'),
    path('add/', views.task_add,
name='task_add'),
```

```python
    path('update/<int:pk>/',
views.task_update,
name='task_update'),
    path('delete/<int:pk>/',
views.task_delete,
name='task_delete'),
]
```

In the main project directory, add an import statement to include the tasks app's URLs in the urls.py file:

```python
python
```

```python
from django.urls import include,
path

urlpatterns = [
    path('admin/',
admin.site.urls),
    path('tasks/',
include('tasks.urls')),
```

]

Conclusion

In this chapter, you learned about Django's core features, why it's ideal for backend development, and how to set it up for the first time. We then created a simple CRUD application where we learned how to define models, set up views, and manage URLs and templates.

With this foundation, you're now ready to explore more advanced topics in Django and start building your own applications. Keep experimenting, and remember—**you've got this!**

Chapter 2: Introduction to React (Frontend)

React is one of the most popular JavaScript libraries used for building user interfaces (UIs), particularly for single-page applications (SPAs). With its component-based architecture and ability to efficiently update and render the user interface, React has revolutionized the way developers approach front-end development. In this chapter, we'll explore what React is, why it's so effective, and guide you step-by-step through the process of setting it up and building your very first React component.

What is React?

At its core, **React** is a JavaScript library used for building dynamic UIs, with a focus on making applications more interactive and responsive. Developed and maintained by Facebook, React allows developers to break down complex UIs into simple, reusable components. Let's break this down further.

Component-Based Architecture

The hallmark feature of React is its **component-based architecture**. A component in React is a building block of a UI—essentially a self-contained unit that can have its own state, properties (props), and logic. Components can be as simple as a button or as complex as an entire form or page layout.

In React, the UI is built by combining these small, reusable components into larger structures. This makes React particularly suited for building dynamic, data-driven applications. With components, you can manage each part of the UI independently, making it easier to update, maintain, and scale applications.

Declarative Syntax

One of React's key features is its declarative approach to UI development. With React, you describe what the UI should look like at any given point in time, and React takes care of updating and rendering the UI when the state changes. This is different from imperative programming, where you would manually define each step to update the UI.

For example, instead of specifying exactly how the UI should change when data updates (like manually manipulating the DOM), React automatically updates the relevant parts of the UI when the underlying data changes.

Virtual DOM

Another important feature of React is the **Virtual DOM**. The Virtual DOM is a lightweight in-memory representation of the actual DOM in the browser. When React components change (due to an event, for example), React first updates the Virtual DOM, then compares it to the actual DOM (a process called **reconciliation**). Only the parts of the DOM that have changed are updated, which significantly improves performance by minimizing direct DOM manipulation.

Unidirectional Data Flow

React uses a **unidirectional data flow** model. This means that data flows in one direction from parent components to child components through **props**. If a component needs to update the data, it can do so by changing its state. The unidirectional flow ensures that the state is predictable and manageable, especially in large applications.

Why Use React?

React offers a host of advantages:

- **Efficient Rendering:** React's Virtual DOM ensures that updates are efficient, resulting in faster applications.

- **Component Reusability:** Components can be reused across different parts of your application, saving time and improving maintainability.

- **Large Ecosystem:** React has a thriving community and an extensive ecosystem, including tools, libraries, and extensions that help developers work more efficiently.

- **Strong Developer Tools:** React provides powerful developer tools, including the React Developer Tools browser extension, which allows you to inspect the component hierarchy and state of your application in real-time.

React is ideal for building dynamic, high-performance UIs for applications, from simple websites to complex, large-scale platforms like Facebook, Instagram, and Netflix.

Setting Up React

Now that we've covered what React is and why it's so powerful, let's dive into setting up React in your development environment. React is very easy to get started with, especially using a tool called **Create React App**. This tool sets up a development environment for you, with all the necessary configurations already taken care of.

Step 1: Install Node.js

React requires **Node.js**, a JavaScript runtime that lets you run JavaScript on the server side. It also includes **npm** (Node Package Manager), which helps you install packages like React.

Here's how to install Node.js:

1. Go to nodejs.org.

2. Download the latest stable version of Node.js.

3. Follow the installation instructions for your operating system.

4. To verify that Node.js and npm are installed, run the following commands in your terminal or command prompt:

```nginx



node -v
npm -v
```

This will print the installed version of Node.js and npm.

Step 2: Install Create React App

Once Node.js is installed, you can install **Create React App**, which will generate a boilerplate React application for you.

To install Create React App, run the following command in your terminal:

```lua
lua
```

```
npm install -g create-react-app
```

This installs the tool globally on your system.

Step 3: Create a New React Project

Now, let's create a new React project. Run the following command:

```sql
sql
```

```
npx create-react-app my-first-app
```

This will create a new directory called my-first-app and generate all the necessary files and folders for your React app. Once the process is complete, navigate into the project directory:

```bash

```

```
cd my-first-app
```

Step 4: Start the Development Server

Now that your project is set up, you can run the development server to view your app in the browser.

Run the following command:

```sql

```

```
npm start
```

This will start the development server, and you should see the default React welcome page at http://localhost:3000 in your browser. Any changes you make to the project files will automatically update in the browser thanks to **hot reloading**.

Building Your First React Component

Now that you have React set up, let's build a simple React component. In this example, we'll create a component that fetches data from a Django backend and displays it in a list.

We'll assume that you already have a Django backend set up and running, which provides a REST API that sends data in JSON format.

Step 1: Creating a New Component

React components are typically stored in the src folder of your project. Let's create a new component called TaskList.

1. In the src folder of your React app, create a new file called TaskList.js.

2. Inside TaskList.js, define a new functional component that will display a list of tasks.

Here's the code for the component:

```javascript
import React, { useState, useEffect } from 'react';

const TaskList = () => {
  const [tasks, setTasks] = useState([]);

  useEffect(() => {
```

```
    // Fetch tasks from the Django
backend API

fetch('http://127.0.0.1:8000/api/t
asks/')  // Adjust the URL to your
Django API endpoint
    .then(response =>
response.json())
    .then(data =>
setTasks(data))
    .catch(error =>
console.error('Error fetching
tasks:', error));
  }, []);

  return (
    <div>
      <h1>Task List</h1>
      <ul>
        {tasks.map(task => (
          <li key={task.id}>
```

```
        {task.title} -
{task.completed ? 'Completed' :
'Pending'}
        </li>
      ))}
      </ul>
    </div>
  );
};


export default TaskList;
```

Step 2: Explaining the Code

Let's break down what's happening in this code:

- **useState:** This hook is used to create state in a functional component. We're using it to store the list of tasks that we fetch from the Django backend.

- **useEffect:** This hook is used to perform side effects in function components. In this case, it's used to fetch data from the Django backend when the component first renders.

- **fetch:** This function is used to make an HTTP request to the Django API. We're fetching the task data as JSON and storing it in the tasks state.

- **map:** We use the map method to loop through the tasks and display each one in a list item (<li>).

Step 3: Rendering the Component

Now that we have the TaskList component, let's render it in the main App.js file.

In src/App.js, import the TaskList component and use it in the JSX:

```javascript


import React from 'react';
```

```
import './App.css';
import TaskList from './TaskList';


function App() {
  return (
    <div className="App">
      <TaskList />
    </div>
  );
}


export default App;
```

Step 4: Testing the Component

Now, run the React app again using npm start, and you should see the task list displayed in your browser, fetched from your Django backend.

Conclusion

In this chapter, you learned about React, its component-based architecture, and how it simplifies the process of building dynamic UIs. You set up a React environment using **Create React App** and created your first React component to display a list of tasks fetched from a Django backend.

React's simplicity, flexibility, and power make it an excellent choice for building front-end applications, and by integrating it with a Django backend, you can create full-stack web applications that are efficient, scalable, and easy to maintain.

Congratulations! You're now ready to continue building more complex React applications and exploring the rich ecosystem of tools and libraries that can help you build amazing things!

Chapter 3: Introduction to Vue.js (Frontend)

Vue.js has become one of the most popular JavaScript frameworks for building dynamic and interactive user interfaces. Known for its simplicity, flexibility, and ease of integration, Vue.js provides an excellent balance between powerful features and developer-friendly syntax. Whether you are new to web development or a seasoned developer, Vue.js makes it easier to create modern, scalable applications. In this chapter, we will explore what Vue.js is, how to set it up, and build your first Vue component. We will also show you how to fetch data from a Django API and display it using Vue.js.

What is Vue.js?

Vue.js is a **progressive JavaScript framework** used for building user interfaces (UIs). What sets Vue apart is its **incremental adoptability**—you can use Vue to handle just the view layer of your application or build full-fledged, complex applications. Vue is designed to be as flexible as possible, allowing you to pick and choose the features that best fit your project.

Key Features of Vue.js:

- **Declarative Rendering:** Vue.js uses declarative rendering to bind the UI to the underlying data model. This allows developers to specify the exact structure of the UI without having to manually manipulate the DOM.

- **Two-Way Data Binding:** Vue uses a two-way data binding mechanism, meaning that changes to the model (data) automatically update the view (UI), and user input in the view automatically updates the model.

- **Component-Based Architecture:** Like React, Vue.js is based on components. Components are reusable and self-contained units that represent UI elements. Components can be combined to build more complex UIs.

- **Directives and Templates:** Vue.js uses a simple syntax with HTML-based templates. It includes built-in directives like v-if, v-for, and v-bind to control rendering, conditional logic, and event handling.

- **Single-File Components (SFC):** Vue's single-file components allow developers to keep HTML, JavaScript, and CSS in one file, making it easier to manage and organize code.

Vue vs. React: A Quick Comparison

Vue.js and React are both used to build dynamic, component-based UIs, but they differ in several ways. Let's explore these differences:

- **Learning Curve:** Vue.js has a much gentler learning curve compared to React. Vue's syntax is easier for beginners to grasp because it uses standard HTML, CSS, and

JavaScript, and it doesn't require understanding concepts like JSX (a JavaScript extension for HTML).

- **Integration:** Vue.js is incredibly flexible and can be used incrementally. You can add Vue to an existing project without needing to rewrite everything, while React often requires a larger upfront commitment. Vue's ease of integration with existing codebases is one of its key strengths.

- **State Management:** React uses **state** and **props** to manage data and interactions, while Vue uses **data** and **props**. However, Vue's **Vuex** library for state management is considered more integrated and easier to use for complex applications.

- **Ecosystem:** React has a larger community and ecosystem compared to Vue, but Vue is growing rapidly and is especially popular in smaller or mid-sized projects due to its simplicity.

- **Performance:** Both frameworks offer excellent performance, but Vue tends to have an edge in terms of **initial rendering** and **update performance** due to its **virtual DOM**.

Setting Up Vue.js

Before you start building with Vue, you need to set it up in your development environment. In this section, we will walk through setting up Vue.js using the **Vue CLI (Command Line Interface)**, which simplifies the process of starting a new project.

Step 1: Install Node.js and npm

Just like with React, you need **Node.js** and **npm** to manage packages in Vue.js.

1. Visit the Node.js download page and download the latest stable version.

2. After installation, verify that Node.js and npm are correctly installed by running:

```bash
```

```bash
node -v
npm -v
```

This will print the installed versions of Node.js and npm.

Step 2: Install Vue CLI

Vue CLI is a command-line tool used to scaffold Vue.js projects. It provides an easy way to set up Vue apps with a single command.

To install Vue CLI globally on your machine, open the terminal and run the following command:

```bash
```

```bash
npm install -g @vue/cli
```

Once installed, you can verify it by running:

```bash
```

```
vue --version
```

Step 3: Create a New Vue Project

Now that Vue CLI is installed, you can create a new Vue project. In your terminal, navigate to the directory where you want to create the project and run:

```bash
```

```
vue create my-first-vue-app
```

Vue CLI will prompt you with some configuration options:

- **Default preset (Babel, ESLint)** is a good choice for beginners.

- You can select other options based on your project needs, like Vue Router or Vuex for state management.

Once Vue CLI finishes setting up the project, navigate into your project directory:

bash

```
cd my-first-vue-app
```

Step 4: Run the Development Server

To view your Vue application, run the development server:

bash

```
npm run serve
```

You should see output similar to this:

arduino

```
App running at:
- Local:    http://localhost:8080/
```

Open http://localhost:8080/ in your browser, and you should see the default Vue.js welcome page.

Creating Your First Vue Component

Now that you have your Vue environment set up, let's create a simple app that fetches data from a **Django API** and displays it in a list. For this example, we'll assume you already have a Django backend running with an **API** endpoint that serves data in JSON format.

Step 1: Create a Vue Component

Vue components are typically stored in the src/components folder. Let's create a component called TaskList.vue.

1. In the src/components folder, create a file named TaskList.vue.

2. Add the following code inside the file:

```vue
<template>
```

```
<div>
  <h1>Task List</h1>
  <ul>
    <li v-for="task in tasks" :key="task.id">
      {{ task.title }} - {{ task.completed ? 'Completed' : 'Pending' }}
    </li>
  </ul>
</div>
</template>

<script>
export default {
  name: 'TaskList',
  data() {
    return {
      tasks: [],
    };
  },
```

```
  mounted() {
    // Fetch tasks from the Django
backend API

fetch('http://127.0.0.1:8000/api/t
asks/')  // Adjust the URL to your
Django API endpoint
      .then(response =>
response.json())
      .then(data => {
        this.tasks = data;
      })
      .catch(error => {
        console.error('Error
fetching tasks:', error);
      });
  },
};
</script>

<style scoped>
```

```css
h1 {
  font-size: 2rem;
  color: #333;
}
ul {
  list-style-type: none;
  padding: 0;
}
li {
  padding: 10px;
  margin-bottom: 5px;
  background-color: #f4f4f4;
  border-radius: 4px;
}
</style>
```

Step 2: Breaking Down the Code

- **Template Section (<template>)**: This is where you define the HTML structure of the component. We use the v-for directive to loop through the tasks array and display each task in a list item (<li>). The :key attribute helps Vue efficiently update the DOM.

- **Script Section (<script>):** In this section, we define the logic for our component. The data() function returns the tasks array, which will store the list of tasks fetched from the Django API. The mounted() lifecycle hook is called when the component is mounted (i.e., when it appears on the screen). It's where we fetch the data using the fetch API.

- **Style Section (<style>):** This section contains the styles for the component. We use scoped to ensure that the styles apply only to this component and not globally.

Step 3: Use the Component in the App

Now that we have the TaskList component, we need to use it in our main App.vue component. Open src/App.vue and update it to include TaskList:

vue

```vue
<template>
  <div id="app">
    <TaskList />
  </div>
</template>

<script>
import TaskList from
'./components/TaskList.vue';

export default {
  name: 'App',
```

```
  components: {
    TaskList,
  },
};
</script>

<style>
/* Global styles */
body {
  font-family: Arial, sans-serif;
  margin: 0;
  padding: 0;
  background-color: #f9f9f9;
}
</style>
```

Step 4: Testing the Application

Run your Vue app with:

```bash
```

```
npm run serve
```

Your application should now display the list of tasks fetched from the Django backend. When you add or modify tasks in your Django API, the Vue.js app will automatically display the updated list.

Conclusion

In this chapter, you learned about Vue.js and its key features, including its **declarative rendering**, **two-way data binding**, and **component-based architecture**. We walked through the process of setting up Vue.js using **Vue CLI**, and created a simple app that fetches data from a Django API and displays it in a Vue component.

Vue's simplicity, flexibility, and power make it an excellent choice for building modern, dynamic UIs. With Vue, you can incrementally adopt new features as your project grows, making it an ideal choice for both small projects and large-scale applications.

You've now built a solid foundation with Vue.js. With this knowledge, you can start building more complex and interactive applications that connect to your backends, create engaging user experiences, and manage state efficiently.

Now, go ahead and experiment with Vue! The possibilities are endless, and as you build more apps, your Vue skills will continue to grow!

Chapter 4: Building the Backend with Django

In this chapter, we will take a deep dive into **Django's powerful backend features**, demonstrating how to build models, views, and templates for a small web application. This chapter will also introduce you to **Django REST Framework (DRF)**, which is a toolkit for creating APIs in Django. With a hands-on approach, we'll go through the creation of models to handle data, views to display content, and templates for rendering HTML. We'll then integrate **Django REST Framework** to expose our backend as a RESTful API, which can easily connect to a frontend, such as a React or Vue.js application.

By the end of this chapter, you will have the skills to:

1. Build models, views, and templates in Django.

2. Create a REST API with **Django REST Framework** to serve data to the frontend.

3. Use Django's admin interface for managing your data models.

Let's get started!

Building Models, Views, and Templates

Django is famous for its ability to handle backend development seamlessly, thanks to its strong model-view-template (MVT) architecture. Understanding this architecture is crucial for building full-fledged applications with Django.

1. Models: Defining the Data Structure

In Django, **models** define the structure of your database. They are Python classes that represent your database tables and are responsible for managing your data, whether it's from a database or any other source. Django makes it easy to interact with databases, eliminating the need for writing SQL queries directly.

Let's imagine we're building a simple **task management application** where users can create tasks, assign them to different people, and track their completion status.

Step 1: Define the Task Model

First, let's define a model for a task in a Django app. In your project directory, navigate to the models.py file inside the app folder (e.g., tasks/models.py) and define a Task model.

```python
from django.db import models


class Task(models.Model):
```

```python
    title =
models.CharField(max_length=100)
# Task title
    description =
models.TextField()   # Task
description
    completed =
models.BooleanField(default=False)
# Completion status
    assigned_to =
models.CharField(max_length=100)
# Person assigned to the task
    due_date =
models.DateTimeField()   # Task due
date

    def __str__(self):
        return self.title
```

Explanation:

- title: A character field to store the name or title of the task.

- description: A text field to store a detailed description of the task.

- completed: A boolean field that marks whether the task is completed.

- assigned_to: A character field to store the name of the person to whom the task is assigned.

- due_date: A datetime field to store the deadline for completing the task.

Once the model is defined, we need to apply the migration to create the database table for the model.

Step 2: Apply Migrations

To apply the migration for your newly created model:

1. Run the following command to create the initial migration:

```bash
bash
```

```bash
python manage.py makemigrations
```

2. Then apply the migration to create the table in your database:

```bash
bash
```

```bash
python manage.py migrate
```

Django will create the necessary database table corresponding to the Task model in the underlying database.

---

2. Views: Handling Logic and Displaying Content

Views in Django are Python functions that receive user requests and return a response. A view typically retrieves data from the model and passes it to the template to display.

For our task management app, let's create views to list all tasks, add a new task, and view details of a single task.

Step 1: Define Views for Task Operations

In the views.py file of your tasks app, define the following views:

python

```python
from django.shortcuts import render, get_object_or_404, redirect
from .models import Task
from .forms import TaskForm

def task_list(request):
    tasks = Task.objects.all()  # Retrieve all tasks
```

```python
    return render(request,
'task_list.html', {'tasks':
tasks})

def task_detail(request, pk):
    task = get_object_or_404(Task,
pk=pk)   # Retrieve task by primary
key (pk)
    return render(request,
'task_detail.html', {'task':
task})

def task_add(request):
    if request.method == 'POST':
        form =
TaskForm(request.POST)
        if form.is_valid():
            form.save()
            return
redirect('task_list')   # Redirect
to task list page
```

```
else:
    form = TaskForm()
return render(request,
'task_form.html', {'form': form})
```

Explanation of Views:

- task_list: Retrieves all the tasks from the database and passes them to the template for rendering.

- task_detail: Retrieves a specific task by its primary key (pk) and passes it to the task_detail.html template.

- task_add: Displays a form to create a new task. When the form is submitted, the task is saved to the database.

3. Templates: Rendering HTML Views

Templates in Django allow you to render dynamic HTML pages that can display data passed from views. Templates are essentially HTML files with placeholders for dynamic data.

Let's create the following templates for our task management app:

Step 1: Create the task_list.html Template

In the templates folder of your app, create the task_list.html template to display all tasks:

html

```
<!DOCTYPE html>
<html lang="en">
<head>
    <meta charset="UTF-8">
```

```html
    <meta name="viewport"
content="width=device-width,
initial-scale=1.0">
    <title>Task List</title>
</head>
<body>
    <h1>Task List</h1>
    <ul>
        {% for task in tasks %}
            <li>
                <a href="{% url
'task_detail' task.pk %}">{{
task.title }}</a> -
                {% if
task.completed %} Completed {%
else %} Pending {% endif %}
            </li>
        {% endfor %}
    </ul>
    <a href="{% url 'task_add'
%}">Add a new task</a>
```

```
</body>
</html>
```

Step 2: Create the task_detail.html Template

Create a template to display the details of a specific task:

html

```
<!DOCTYPE html>
<html lang="en">
<head>
    <meta charset="UTF-8">
    <meta name="viewport"
content="width=device-width,
initial-scale=1.0">
    <title>{{ task.title
}}</title>
</head>
<body>
    <h1>{{ task.title }}</h1>
    <p>{{ task.description }}</p>
```

```
    <p>Assigned to: {{
task.assigned_to }}</p>
    <p>Due date: {{ task.due_date
}}</p>
    <p>Status: {% if
task.completed %} Completed {%
else %} Pending {% endif %}</p>
    <a href="{% url 'task_list'
%}">Back to Task List</a>
</body>
</html>
```

Step 3: Create the task_form.html Template

Finally, let's create a template for adding a new task:

```
html
```

```html
<!DOCTYPE html>
<html lang="en">
<head>
    <meta charset="UTF-8">
```

```html
    <meta name="viewport"
content="width=device-width,
initial-scale=1.0">
    <title>Add New Task</title>
</head>
<body>
    <h1>Add New Task</h1>
    <form method="post">
        {% csrf_token %}
        {{ form.as_p }}
        <button
type="submit">Save</button>
    </form>
    <a href="{% url 'task_list'
%}">Back to Task List</a>
</body>
</html>
```

Django REST Framework (DRF)

Now that we have models, views, and templates set up, it's time to make our app more dynamic and frontend-friendly by creating an API using **Django REST Framework (DRF)**.

1. Installing Django REST Framework

To get started with DRF, first, you need to install it. Run the following command:

bash

```bash
pip install djangorestframework
```

Once installed, add 'rest_framework' to your INSTALLED_APPS in the settings.py file:

python

```python
INSTALLED_APPS = [
    ...,
    'rest_framework',
]
```

2. Creating Serializers

In Django, serializers are responsible for converting model instances to JSON format, which can be easily used in APIs.

Let's create a serializer for our Task model. Create a new file tasks/serializers.py:

python

```python
from rest_framework import serializers
from .models import Task

class TaskSerializer(serializers.ModelSerializer):
    class Meta:
        model = Task
        fields = '__all__'  # Include all fields from the Task model
```

3. Creating API Views

Now let's create views for our API. You can use **class-based views** provided by DRF to handle standard API operations like listing, retrieving, creating, updating, and deleting data.

In tasks/views.py, add the following API views:

python

```python
from rest_framework import generics
from .models import Task
from .serializers import TaskSerializer


class TaskList(generics.ListCreateAPIView):
    queryset = Task.objects.all()
    serializer_class = TaskSerializer
```

```
class
TaskDetail(generics.RetrieveUpdate
DestroyAPIView):
    queryset = Task.objects.all()
    serializer_class =
TaskSerializer
```

- TaskList: This view handles both listing all tasks and creating a new task.

- TaskDetail: This view allows you to retrieve, update, or delete a task by its primary key.

4. Setting Up URLs for the API

In the tasks/urls.py file, set up the URLs for the API:

```python

from django.urls import path
from . import views

```

```
urlpatterns = [
    path('api/tasks/',
views.TaskList.as_view(),
name='task_list_api'),
    path('api/tasks/<int:pk>/',
views.TaskDetail.as_view(),
name='task_detail_api'),
]
```

Conclusion

In this chapter, we built a **task management app** using Django's powerful backend features, including models, views, and templates. We also created a REST API using **Django REST Framework** to expose the backend data to the frontend.

By learning how to build models to handle data, views to handle logic, templates to render

HTML, and APIs to connect with frontend technologies, you now have a full understanding of Django's capabilities for backend development.

You're ready to dive deeper into building more complex and dynamic applications, integrating Django with frontend technologies like **React** or **Vue.js**, and utilizing Django REST Framework to create flexible and powerful APIs.

Keep experimenting with Django—**you've got this!**

Chapter 5: Connecting Django with React

In this chapter, we'll bridge the gap between the Django backend and the React frontend. This is an essential skill when building modern web applications, as it enables you to fetch and display data from the Django backend in your React components. We'll walk through fetching data from Django's API endpoints, managing that data efficiently in React, and ensuring smooth, dynamic interactions in your application.

By the end of this chapter, you will:

- Learn how to connect Django with React by fetching data from Django's API.

- Understand how to manage state in React to handle dynamic updates to your application.

- Explore best practices for handling data in large applications with React's state management.

Let's dive in!

Fetching Data with React

Fetching data from a backend is one of the most common tasks in modern web development. In this section, we will guide you through how to connect React to Django's API endpoints and fetch data asynchronously. We will use **Django REST Framework (DRF)** as the API for the backend and use **React's built-in fetch function** to retrieve the data.

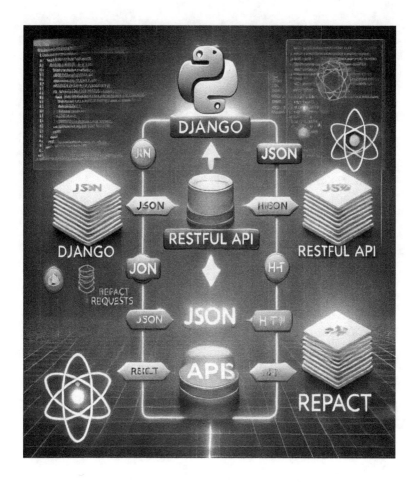

Step 1: Setting Up Django API Endpoints

Before we can fetch data in React, let's ensure that the Django backend is ready to provide data through API endpoints. In Chapter 4, we set up basic API views using Django REST Framework

(DRF). Here's a quick recap of how to set up your Django API to expose task data:

python

```python
# tasks/views.py
from rest_framework import generics
from .models import Task
from .serializers import TaskSerializer


class TaskList(generics.ListCreateAPIView):
    queryset = Task.objects.all()
    serializer_class = TaskSerializer


class TaskDetail(generics.RetrieveUpdateDestroyAPIView):
```

```python
    queryset = Task.objects.all()
    serializer_class =
TaskSerializer
```

Make sure the following URLs are set up for the API:

```python

# tasks/urls.py
from django.urls import path
from . import views

urlpatterns = [
    path('api/tasks/',
views.TaskList.as_view(),
name='task_list_api'),
    path('api/tasks/<int:pk>/',
views.TaskDetail.as_view(),
name='task_detail_api'),
]
```

These API endpoints will allow React to retrieve the list of tasks and individual task details.

Step 2: Setting Up React for Data Fetching

Now let's set up the React frontend to fetch data from the Django backend. We'll be using **React's fetch function** to asynchronously fetch data from the Django API.

Creating a React Component to Fetch Data

Let's create a simple TaskList component in React that will fetch the list of tasks from the Django API and display them.

1. **Create the TaskList Component**: In your React project, create a new file called TaskList.js in the src directory (or components folder, if you have one). Here's how you can set up the component:

javascript

```
import React, { useState,
useEffect } from 'react';

const TaskList = () => {
  // State to store tasks
  const [tasks, setTasks] =
useState([]);

  // Fetch data when the component
mounts
  useEffect(() => {

fetch('http://127.0.0.1:8000/api/t
asks/')
    .then(response =>
response.json())
    .then(data =>
setTasks(data))
```

```
      .catch(error =>
console.error('Error fetching
tasks:', error));
  }, []);

  return (
    <div>
      <h1>Task List</h1>
      <ul>
        {tasks.map(task => (
          <li key={task.id}>
            {task.title} -
{task.completed ? 'Completed' :
'Pending'}
          </li>
        ))}
      </ul>
    </div>
  );
};
```

```
export default TaskList;
```

Explanation:

- **useState**: We use useState to manage the list of tasks. Initially, it's set to an empty array.

- **useEffect**: The useEffect hook is used to fetch the data as soon as the component mounts. The empty dependency array ([]) ensures that the fetch operation only runs once, similar to componentDidMount in class components.

- **fetch**: We use fetch to make a GET request to the Django API (http://127.0.0.1:8000/api/tasks/). The response is parsed as JSON and stored in the tasks state using setTasks.

Displaying the Data

Inside the component's JSX, we map through the tasks array and render each task as a list item. We also display the task's title and completion status (either "Completed" or "Pending").

Step 3: Displaying the TaskList Component in the App

Now that we have the TaskList component, let's render it in the main App.js file. Open src/App.js and modify it like this:

```javascript
import React from 'react';
import TaskList from './TaskList';

function App() {
  return (
    <div className="App">
      <TaskList />
    </div>
```

```
  );
}
```

```
export default App;
```

Now, when you run the app using npm start, the tasks will be fetched from Django's API and displayed in your React app.

State Management with React

One of the most powerful features of React is its ability to manage state efficiently. Managing state correctly is crucial, especially in large applications where data changes frequently. In this section, we will dive into React's state management techniques and explore how to handle complex data and interactions.

1. Understanding React State

State in React is used to store data that affects the rendering of a component. When the state of a component changes, React re-renders the component to reflect the changes. This allows the user interface to stay in sync with the data.

There are two main types of state in React:

- **Local State**: This state is specific to a component and is managed using the useState hook or the this.state object in class components.

- **Global State**: This state can be accessed across multiple components and is usually managed by state management libraries like **Redux** or **Context API**.

2. Using useState for Local State

Let's revisit our TaskList component to see how useState works. The state in the component holds the list of tasks, and React automatically re-renders the component when the state is updated.

Example of Managing Local State:

javascript

```javascript
const [tasks, setTasks] =
useState([]);
```

Here, tasks is the state variable, and setTasks is the function used to update that state. Initially, tasks is an empty array, and we update it once the data is fetched from the API.

3. Managing More Complex Data with State

As applications grow, you may need to manage more complex data or multiple pieces of state. React provides hooks and patterns to efficiently manage this complexity.

Example of Managing Multiple State Variables:

```javascript
javascript

const [tasks, setTasks] =
useState([]);
const [loading, setLoading] =
useState(true);
```

```
const [error, setError] =
useState(null);
```

In this example:

- tasks stores the list of tasks.

- loading is a boolean flag that tracks whether the data is still being fetched.

- error stores any error that occurs during the fetch operation.

Updating State Based on Previous State

Sometimes, the new state depends on the previous state. In such cases, you can use the callback form of setState.

```javascript
setTasks(prevTasks =>
[...prevTasks, newTask]);
```

This ensures that the new state is based on the previous state, which is especially useful when adding or updating items in a list.

4. Using Context API for Global State Management

For managing state that needs to be accessed across multiple components, the **Context API** is an excellent built-in solution. The Context API allows you to create a global state that can be shared by any component without passing props manually.

Example of Using Context API for Global State:

First, create a context:

```javascript
import React, { createContext, useState } from 'react';
```

```javascript
export const TaskContext =
createContext();


export const TaskProvider = ({
children }) => {
  const [tasks, setTasks] =
useState([]);
  return (
    <TaskContext.Provider value={{
tasks, setTasks }}>
      {children}
    </TaskContext.Provider>
  );
};
```

Now wrap your app with the TaskProvider in App.js:

```javascript
javascript


import React from 'react';
import { TaskProvider } from
'./TaskContext';
```

```
import TaskList from './TaskList';

function App() {
  return (
    <TaskProvider>
      <TaskList />
    </TaskProvider>
  );
}


export default App;
```

To use the state in a component, you can use useContext:

```javascript

import React, { useContext } from
'react';
import { TaskContext } from
'./TaskContext';

const TaskList = () => {
```

```
  const { tasks } =
useContext(TaskContext);
  return (
    <div>
      <h1>Task List</h1>
      <ul>
        {tasks.map(task => (
          <li key={task.id}>
            {task.title} -
{task.completed ? 'Completed' :
'Pending'}
          </li>
        ))}
      </ul>
    </div>
  );
};
```

This allows you to access the tasks state from anywhere in the app.

5. Advanced State Management with Redux

For large applications with more complex state management needs, **Redux** is a popular choice. Redux is a state management library that helps maintain the global state in a predictable manner.

Although Redux is powerful, it adds complexity and is often overkill for smaller applications. We won't dive into Redux in this chapter, but it's something you can explore once you're comfortable with React's built-in state management tools.

Conclusion

In this chapter, we explored how to connect a Django backend to a React frontend by fetching data from Django's API. We used React's fetch function to retrieve task data and displayed it in a component. Additionally, we covered React's state management, from local state using useState to managing more complex data using Context API.

By mastering data fetching and state management in React, you're now equipped to build dynamic, interactive applications that can efficiently handle and display data from a backend server. As you continue to build with React, you'll gain a deeper understanding of how to manage state, handle asynchronous data, and scale your applications effectively.

You've made great progress—**keep up the great work!**

Chapter 6: Connecting Django with Vue.js

In this chapter, we will walk through the process of connecting a **Django backend** with a **Vue.js frontend** to create a modern web application. By the end of this chapter, you will have learned how to create **Vue.js components**, bind data from Django's API to those components, handle user interactions, and manage routing with **Vue Router**. The combination of Django and Vue.js allows you to build powerful, dynamic web applications that are responsive, scalable, and easy to maintain.

Let's break this chapter down into two main sections:

1. **Vue.js Components and Data Binding** – Learn how to create Vue components and bind data from Django's API.

2. **Vue Router for Navigation** – Discover how to use Vue Router to manage navigation in a multi-page app.

Vue.js Components and Data Binding

Vue.js is a flexible and powerful JavaScript framework that allows developers to create dynamic UIs with ease. One of the main features that make Vue.js stand out is its **component-based architecture**. Components in Vue.js are reusable, self-contained pieces of the UI, each managing its own state and behavior.

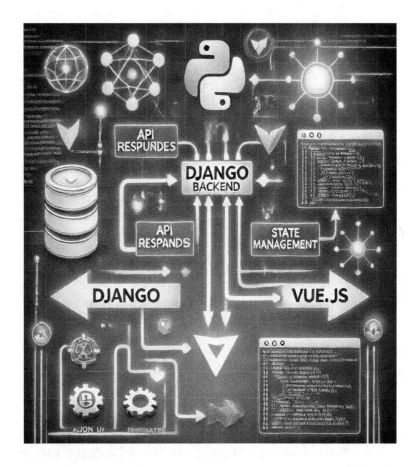

1. Setting Up Vue.js

Before diving into creating components and binding data, we need to set up a Vue.js project that will connect to Django's **API**. To get started, we will use **Vue CLI**, a command-line tool that sets up Vue.js projects with preconfigured settings.

Step 1: Install Vue CLI

If you don't have Vue CLI installed, you can do so by running:

bash

```
npm install -g @vue/cli
```

Step 2: Create a New Vue Project

Once Vue CLI is installed, create a new project by running:

bash

```
vue create vue-django-app
```

Follow the prompts to select the features you want, and once the project is created, navigate to the project folder:

bash

```
cd vue-django-app
```

Step 3: Run the Development Server

Now, run the development server to see the Vue.js app in action:

```
bash
```

```
npm run serve
```

Your Vue app should now be live at http://localhost:8080/.

---

2. Creating Vue Components

In Vue.js, components are the building blocks of your application. Each component encapsulates the logic, template, and styling for a specific part of your app. Let's start by creating a simple **TaskList** component that will fetch data from Django's API.

Step 1: Create the TaskList.vue Component

In the src/components/ directory, create a new file called TaskList.vue. This component will be responsible for displaying a list of tasks fetched from Django's backend API.

vue

```
<template>
  <div>
    <h1>Task List</h1>
    <ul>
      <li v-for="task in tasks"
:key="task.id">
        {{ task.title }} -
        <span v-
if="task.completed">Completed</spa
n>
        <span v-
else>Pending</span>
      </li>
```

```
    </ul>
   </div>
</template>

<script>
export default {
  name: 'TaskList',
  data() {
    return {
      tasks: [],
    };
  },
  mounted() {
    this.fetchTasks();
  },
  methods: {
    fetchTasks() {

fetch('http://127.0.0.1:8000/api/t
asks/')   // Django API endpoint
```

```
        .then(response =>
response.json())
        .then(data => {
          this.tasks = data;
        })
        .catch(error => {
          console.error('Error
fetching tasks:', error);
        });
    },
  },
};
</script>

<style scoped>
h1 {
  color: #333;
}
ul {
  list-style-type: none;
  padding: 0;
```

```css
}
li {
  padding: 10px;
  margin-bottom: 5px;
  background-color: #f4f4f4;
  border-radius: 5px;
}
</style>
```

Explanation:

- **Template Section:** The template contains an unordered list (<ul>) that iterates over the tasks array using the v-for directive. It displays the title and status of each task, whether it's completed or pending.

- **Script Section:**

  - **data:** Defines a tasks array to store the fetched tasks.

  - **mounted:** The mounted lifecycle hook calls fetchTasks when the component is first created, ensuring that the tasks are fetched as soon as the component is loaded.

- o **fetchTasks**: This method fetches data from the Django backend's API (http://127.0.0.1:8000/api/tasks/) and updates the tasks state.

- **Style Section**: Adds some basic styling to make the task list look clean and presentable.

Step 2: Using the TaskList Component

To render this component in your app, you need to import and use it in the App.vue component.

1. Open src/App.vue and modify it as follows:

```vue

<template>
  <div id="app">
```

```
    <TaskList />
  </div>
</template>

<script>
import TaskList from
'./components/TaskList.vue';

export default {
  name: 'App',
  components: {
    TaskList,
  },
};
</script>

<style>
#app {
  font-family: 'Arial', sans-
serif;
  margin: 20px;
```

```
}
</style>
```

Now when you run the app, it should display the task list fetched from your Django backend.

---

3. Vue.js Data Binding

Vue.js provides a powerful system for **two-way data binding**. This allows you to easily bind data between the model (JavaScript) and the view (HTML). This concept is critical for ensuring that changes to the data in your JavaScript code automatically reflect in the UI and vice versa.

Step 1: Two-Way Data Binding

To demonstrate Vue's two-way data binding, let's add a feature where users can mark tasks as completed or pending. We will update the TaskList.vue component to allow the user to toggle the completion status of tasks.

Here's how you can modify the task list to include a button for toggling the task's completion status:

vue

```
<template>
  <div>
    <h1>Task List</h1>
    <ul>
      <li v-for="task in tasks"
:key="task.id">
        {{ task.title }} -
        <span v-
if="task.completed">Completed</spa
n>
        <span v-
else>Pending</span>
        <button
@click="toggleCompletion(task)">To
ggle Status</button>
      </li>
    </ul>
```

```
    </div>
</template>

<script>
export default {
  name: 'TaskList',
  data() {
    return {
      tasks: [],
    };
  },
  mounted() {
    this.fetchTasks();
  },
  methods: {
    fetchTasks() {

fetch('http://127.0.0.1:8000/api/t
asks/')
        .then(response =>
response.json())
```

```
    .then(data => {
       this.tasks = data;
    })
    .catch(error => {
       console.error('Error
fetching tasks:', error);
    });
  },
  toggleCompletion(task) {
    task.completed =
!task.completed;  // Toggle the
completed status
    },
  },
};
</script>
```

Explanation:

- **toggleCompletion**: This method toggles the completed status of the task whenever the button is clicked.

- **Button (<button>):** Each task has a button that, when clicked, calls the toggleCompletion method.

This is an example of Vue's two-way data binding, where changing the state of a variable (in this case, task.completed) automatically updates the view.

Vue Router for Navigation

In modern web applications, navigation is a key aspect, especially when building single-page applications (SPAs). Vue Router is the official routing library for Vue.js, and it allows you to manage navigation between different pages or views in your application.

1. Installing Vue Router

To set up Vue Router in your Vue.js project, you need to install it first:

```bash

npm install vue-router
```

2. Setting Up Vue Router

Once installed, you can configure Vue Router in your project.

Step 1: Create Routes

First, create two views: one for the task list and one for task details. In the src/views/ directory, create the following files:

- TaskListView.vue (for the task list)

- TaskDetailView.vue (for displaying the details of a specific task)

Here's an example of how to create TaskListView.vue:

vue

```
<template>
  <div>
    <h1>Task List</h1>
    <TaskList />
```

```
    </div>
</template>

<script>
import TaskList from
'../components/TaskList.vue';

export default {
  name: 'TaskListView',
  components: {
    TaskList,
  },
};
</script>
```

And for TaskDetailView.vue, we can create a simple template to display a single task's details:

vue

```
<template>
  <div>
    <h1>Task Detail</h1>
```

```
  <p>Task details will be
displayed here.</p>
  </div>
</template>

<script>
export default {
  name: 'TaskDetailView',
};
</script>
```

Step 2: Configure the Router

Now, create a new file src/router/index.js to configure the routes:

```javascript
import Vue from 'vue';
import Router from 'vue-router';
import TaskListView from
'../views/TaskListView.vue';
```

```
import TaskDetailView from
'../views/TaskDetailView.vue';

Vue.use(Router);

export default new Router({
  routes: [
    {
      path: '/',
      name: 'task-list',
      component: TaskListView,
    },
    {
      path: '/task/:id',
      name: 'task-detail',
      component: TaskDetailView,
      props: true,
    },
  ],
});
```

In this setup:

- The root path (/) will display the TaskListView.

- A dynamic path (/task/:id) will display the TaskDetailView and pass the task's id as a prop.

Step 3: Using Router in the App

Finally, configure the router in src/main.js:

```javascript
import Vue from 'vue';
import App from './App.vue';
import router from './router';

Vue.config.productionTip = false;

new Vue({
  render: h => h(App),
  router,
}).$mount('#app');
```

Step 4: Adding Navigation Links

Now, add navigation links to switch between pages. You can update the TaskList.vue component to include links to the task detail page.

vue

```
<template>
  <div>
    <h1>Task List</h1>
    <ul>
      <li v-for="task in tasks"
:key="task.id">
        <router-link :to="'/task/'
+ task.id">{{ task.title
}}</router-link> -
        <span v-
if="task.completed">Completed</spa
n>
```

```
    <span v-
else>Pending</span>
    </li>
  </ul>
 </div>
</template>
```

The router-link component allows navigation to different routes without reloading the page.

Conclusion

In this chapter, you learned how to:

- Create **Vue.js components** and bind data fetched from Django's API using **Vue.js' two-way data binding**.

- Manage dynamic user interactions like toggling task completion.

- Set up **Vue Router** to handle navigation and build a multi-page app.

You now have the tools to build a fully dynamic and interactive frontend with Vue.js, fetching and displaying data from a Django backend. This is just the beginning; as you continue to explore more advanced Vue.js features, you'll be able to build even more complex applications with ease.

Great job! You're well on your way to mastering **Vue.js** and **Django** for full-stack development.

Chapter 7: Authentication and Authorization

Authentication and authorization are crucial aspects of modern web applications. **Authentication** ensures that users are who they say they are, while **authorization** controls what they can access within the application. In this chapter, we'll dive into setting up **user authentication** using **Django's built-in tools** and **third-party libraries**, and we'll also cover how to **secure the frontend** (React/Vue) to handle authentication safely.

By the end of this chapter, you will:

- Learn how to implement user authentication in Django using its built-in tools and third-party libraries like **django-allauth**.

- Understand how to securely handle authentication in the frontend using **React** or **Vue.js**.

- Be able to manage sessions or tokens securely to maintain a seamless user experience.

User Authentication with Django

Django provides built-in support for user authentication, including tools for handling user login, registration, and password management. It's highly customizable, so you can easily extend it with additional functionality to meet your needs.

1. Setting Up Authentication in Django

Let's start by setting up basic authentication using Django's built-in tools. We'll walk through the process of creating user accounts, managing logins, and adding user registration to our app.

Step 1: Enable Django Authentication

Django comes with a built-in user authentication system that includes login, logout, and session management. To use Django's authentication system, ensure you have 'django.contrib.auth' and 'django.contrib.sessions' included in your **INSTALLED_APPS** in the settings.py file. Django also provides middleware to manage user sessions.

python

```python
INSTALLED_APPS = [
    'django.contrib.auth',
    'django.contrib.sessions',
    'django.contrib.contenttypes',
    'django.contrib.messages',
    # other apps
]
```

Step 2: Creating a User Model

If you need a custom user model (e.g., adding extra fields), you can extend Django's default User model. To create a custom user model, add the following to your models.py file:

```python

from django.contrib.auth.models
import AbstractUser
from django.db import models

class CustomUser(AbstractUser):
    birthdate =
models.DateField(null=True,
blank=True)
    # Add other custom fields if
needed
```

Then, inform Django that you are using a custom user model by *updating the AUTH_USER_MODEL setting in settings.py:*

python

AUTH_USER_MODEL = 'yourapp.CustomUser'

Step 3: Setting Up User Registration, Login, and Logout Views

Django provides built-in views and forms for handling user registration, login, and logout. However, we will create custom views to handle these actions, making our app more flexible.

For example, let's create a **user registration view** in views.py:

python

```
from django.shortcuts import render, redirect
```

```python
from django.contrib.auth.forms
import UserCreationForm
from django.contrib.auth import
login


def register(request):
    if request.method == 'POST':
        form =
UserCreationForm(request.POST)
        if form.is_valid():
            user = form.save()
            login(request, user)
# Automatically log in the user
after registration
            return
redirect('home')  # Redirect to
the homepage after successful
registration
    else:
        form = UserCreationForm()
```

```
    return render(request,
'registration/register.html',
{'form': form})
```

In urls.py, add the path for the registration view:

python

```
from django.urls import path
from .views import register

urlpatterns = [
    path('register/', register,
name='register'),
]
```

Step 4: Django Login and Logout Views

Django also comes with built-in views for handling login and logout. You can use these views directly, or customize them if needed. To set up login, add the following URL patterns:

python

```
from django.contrib.auth import
views as auth_views

urlpatterns = [
    path('login/',
auth_views.LoginView.as_view(),
name='login'),
    path('logout/',
auth_views.LogoutView.as_view(),
name='logout'),
]
```

By default, Django will look for login.html and logged_out.html templates in your templates/registration/ folder. You can customize these templates to match your design.

2. Using Third-Party Authentication Tools

While Django's built-in tools are powerful, sometimes you might want to add more advanced features like social authentication (e.g., login with Google, Facebook, etc.). **django-allauth** is a third-party library that integrates with Django to provide a comprehensive authentication system, including social login.

Step 1: Installing django-allauth

To add social authentication to your app, you can use django-allauth. First, install it via pip:

```bash
```

```bash
pip install django-allauth
```

Step 2: Configuring django-allauth

Add the following apps to INSTALLED_APPS in settings.py:

```python
python
```

```python
INSTALLED_APPS = [
    'django.contrib.sites',
    'django.contrib.auth',
    'allauth',
    'allauth.account',
    'allauth.socialaccount',
    # other apps
]
```

Add the following authentication backends to **AUTHENTICATION_BACKENDS:**

```python
python
```

```python
AUTHENTICATION_BACKENDS = (

'allauth.account.auth_backends.Aut
henticationBackend',
)
```

Set up **SITE_ID:**

python

```
SITE_ID = 1
```

Include the URLs for authentication in your urls.py:

python

```
from django.urls import path, include

urlpatterns = [
    path('accounts/', include('allauth.urls')),
]
```

After these changes, django-allauth will provide views for login, registration, and social authentication (Google, Facebook, etc.).

Securing the React/Vue Frontend

Once your Django backend is set up to handle authentication, it's important to ensure that the **frontend** securely manages user sessions or tokens. In this section, we will walk through how to handle authentication in React or Vue.js, specifically focusing on **session management** and **JWT (JSON Web Token)**.

1. Securing Authentication with JWT

JWT is a widely-used method of securing authentication in modern web applications. After a user logs in, Django can issue a JWT that the frontend stores and uses for subsequent API requests.

Step 1: Installing djangorestframework-simplejwt

First, we need to install **djangorestframework-simplejwt**, a simple JWT authentication library for Django:

```bash
bash
```

```bash
pip install djangorestframework-
simplejwt
```

In your settings.py, configure JWT authentication:

```python
python
```

```
INSTALLED_APPS = [
    # other apps
    'rest_framework_simplejwt',
]


REST_FRAMEWORK = {


'DEFAULT_AUTHENTICATION_CLASSES':
(


'rest_framework_simplejwt.authenti
cation.JWTAuthentication',
    ),
}
```

Step 2: Set Up JWT Views in Django

Now, let's create views for obtaining and refreshing JWT tokens in your urls.py:

```python
python
```

```
from
rest_framework_simplejwt.views
import TokenObtainPairView,
TokenRefreshView

urlpatterns = [
    path('api/token/',
TokenObtainPairView.as_view(),
name='token_obtain_pair'),
    path('api/token/refresh/',
TokenRefreshView.as_view(),
name='token_refresh'),
]
```

The TokenObtainPairView provides an endpoint for obtaining a JWT pair (access and refresh tokens), and TokenRefreshView allows users to refresh their access token using a valid refresh token.

Step 3: Handling Authentication in React/Vue

Now, let's handle the JWT authentication on the frontend.

In React:

To store and send the JWT in requests, you will use **localStorage** (or **cookies** for added security) to store the token and include it in the **Authorization** header of API requests.

1. **Login Form in React**: Create a login form component that will send the username and password to the backend to get the JWT token.

```javascript
import React, { useState } from 'react';

const LoginForm = () => {
```

```
const [username, setUsername] =
useState('');
const [password, setPassword] =
useState('');
const [error, setError] =
useState('');


const handleSubmit = (e) => {
    e.preventDefault();



fetch('http://127.0.0.1:8000/api/t
oken/', {
        method: 'POST',
        body: JSON.stringify({
username, password }),
        headers: { 'Content-Type':
'application/json' },
    })
    .then(res => res.json())
    .then(data => {
```

```
    if (data.access) {

localStorage.setItem('access_token
', data.access);
        // Redirect to the
dashboard or homepage
      } else {
        setError('Invalid
credentials');
      }
    })
    .catch(error =>
setError('Login failed'));
  };

  return (
    <form onSubmit={handleSubmit}>
      <input
        type="text"
        placeholder="Username"
        value={username}
```

```
        onChange={(e) =>
setUsername(e.target.value)}
        />
        <input
          type="password"
          placeholder="Password"
          value={password}
          onChange={(e) =>
setPassword(e.target.value)}
        />
        <button
type="submit">Login</button>
        {error && <p>{error}</p>}
      </form>
    );
};


export default LoginForm;
```

2. **Making Authenticated API Requests**: Whenever making authenticated requests, add the token to the **Authorization header**:

```javascript
javascript

const token =
localStorage.getItem('access_token
');

fetch('http://127.0.0.1:8000/api/t
asks/', {
  headers: {
    'Authorization': `Bearer
${token}`,
  },
})
.then(res => res.json())
.then(data => console.log(data));
```

In Vue.js:

The process is similar in Vue.js. Here's how to handle login and token storage:

1. **Login Component:**

```vue
vue
```

```
<template>
  <div>
    <form @submit.prevent="login">
      <input v-model="username"
placeholder="Username" />
      <input v-model="password"
type="password"
placeholder="Password" />
      <button
type="submit">Login</button>
    </form>
    <p v-if="error">{{ error
}}</p>
  </div>
</template>

<script>
export default {
  data() {
    return {
```

```
      username: '',
      password: '',
      error: '',
    };
  },
  methods: {
    login() {

fetch('http://127.0.0.1:8000/api/t
oken/', {
        method: 'POST',
        headers: { 'Content-Type':
'application/json' },
        body: JSON.stringify({
          username: this.username,
          password: this.password,
        }),
      })
      .then(response =>
response.json())
      .then(data => {
```

```
if (data.access) {

localStorage.setItem('access_token
', data.access);
        // Redirect to another
page or update the UI
        } else {
        this.error = 'Invalid
credentials';
        }
      });
    },
  },
};
</script>
```

2. **Making Authenticated API Requests**: Just like in React, use the token for authentication in Vue.js API requests.

javascript

```
const token =
localStorage.getItem('access_token
');

fetch('http://127.0.0.1:8000/api/t
asks/', {
  headers: {
    'Authorization': `Bearer
${token}`,
  },
})
.then(response => response.json())
.then(data => console.log(data));
```

Conclusion

In this chapter, you learned how to handle **user authentication** and **authorization** in Django using its built-in tools and third-party libraries like **django-allauth**. You also explored how to **secure**

the frontend in React and Vue.js by storing and managing **JWT tokens** for authentication.

This knowledge is critical for building secure, user-friendly applications. By applying these concepts, you can ensure that your web application has strong user authentication and secure data handling, while also offering a smooth and responsive frontend experience.

You've made great progress—keep going and continue building secure, powerful applications! **You've got this!**

Chapter 8: Optimizing the Full-Stack Application

As you build a full-stack application, the need for **performance optimization** becomes more apparent. A well-optimized application can handle more users, perform faster, and provide a better user experience. In this chapter, we'll explore **performance tuning strategies** for both **Django** (the backend) and **React/Vue.js** (the frontend). We will discuss techniques like **caching, database indexing, query optimization, lazy loading, code splitting,** and **memoization** to ensure that your full-stack application runs efficiently.

By the end of this chapter, you will:

- Learn how to optimize Django's performance using caching, database indexing, and efficient query techniques.

- Discover how to optimize React and Vue.js performance with techniques like lazy loading, code splitting, and memoization.

- Apply these optimizations to a full-stack application, improving both backend and frontend performance.

Let's dive in!

Performance Tuning with Django

Django is a powerful web framework that can be optimized to handle large-scale applications efficiently. Whether you're running a small personal project or a large enterprise application, optimizing your Django app's performance will help it run smoothly and handle more traffic.

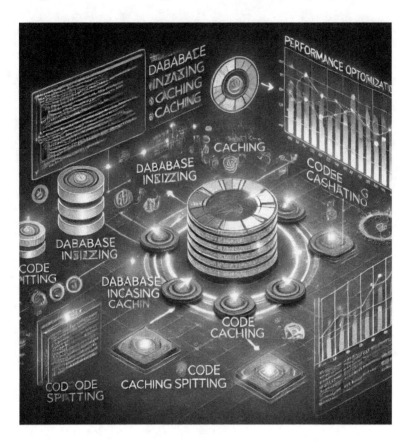

1. Caching in Django

Caching is one of the most effective ways to speed up a Django application. It allows you to store the results of expensive computations or database queries in memory so they can be reused without redoing the work. Django provides multiple caching strategies to choose from.

Step 1: Using Django's Cache Framework

Django includes a **cache framework** that supports various caching backends like **Memcached** and **Redis**. Let's start by configuring caching in Django.

1. **Install a Cache Backend**: For this example, we'll use **Memcached**. Install it by running:

bash

```
pip install python-memcached
```

Configure Caching: In settings.py, configure your caching backend as follows:

python

```
CACHES = {
    'default': {
```

```
        'BACKEND':
'django.core.cache.backends.memcac
hed.MemcachedCache',
        'LOCATION':
'127.0.0.1:11211',
    }
}
```

2. **Use Caching in Views**: To cache the result of a view, you can use Django's cache_page decorator.

Example:

python

```
from django.views.decorators.cache
import cache_page
from django.shortcuts import
render


@cache_page(60 * 15)  # Cache the
view for 15 minutes
```

```python
def my_view(request):
    data = expensive_query()  #
Some database query or heavy
computation
    return render(request,
'template.html', {'data': data})
```

Step 2: Cache Database Queries

If you have expensive database queries, you can cache the results to avoid querying the database every time.

python

```python
from django.core.cache import
cache
from .models import Task

def get_tasks():
    tasks = cache.get('tasks')
    if not tasks:
```

```
    tasks = Task.objects.all()
# Database query
        cache.set('tasks', tasks,
timeout=60*15)   # Cache for 15
minutes
    return tasks
```

This ensures that the query result is cached for 15 minutes and doesn't hit the database every time the function is called.

---

2. Database Indexing

Database indexing is a powerful technique for speeding up database queries, especially when working with large datasets. Indexes improve the speed of data retrieval operations, but they also add some overhead when inserting or updating data.

Step 1: Adding Indexes to Models

Django allows you to create indexes on your model fields. By default, Django adds indexes to primary key fields, but you can manually add indexes to other fields as needed.

Example of adding an index:

```python
from django.db import models

class Task(models.Model):
    title =
models.CharField(max_length=100)
    due_date =
models.DateTimeField()

    class Meta:
        indexes = [

models.Index(fields=['due_date']),
```

```
# Add an index on the 'due_date'
field
        ]
```

Step 2: Using Unique and Foreign Key Indexes

Django automatically creates indexes on ForeignKey and Unique fields, but you can explicitly declare them in the Meta class if needed:

python

```python
class Task(models.Model):
    user = models.ForeignKey(User,
on_delete=models.CASCADE)
    title =
models.CharField(max_length=100,
unique=True)  # Unique field index
```

This helps ensure that lookups on these fields are faster.

3. Query Optimization

Django's ORM is powerful, but it can sometimes result in inefficient database queries. By optimizing your queries, you can reduce the load on the database and speed up the application.

Step 1: Using select_related and prefetch_related

If you are querying related models (i.e., foreign keys, many-to-many relationships), Django will by default run a new query for each related model. This can lead to unnecessary database hits, which can be optimized using select_related and prefetch_related.

- **select_related**: Use this for **ForeignKey** and **OneToOne** relationships to fetch related data in a single query.

Example:

python

```
tasks =
Task.objects.select_related('user'
).all()  # Optimizes database
queries
```

- **prefetch_related**: Use this for **ManyToMany** relationships or when you need to query multiple related objects.

Example:

python

```
tasks =
Task.objects.prefetch_related('tag
s').all()
```

Step 2: Limiting Querysets

Sometimes you only need a subset of data. Using Django's ORM methods like .only() or .values(), you can limit the data retrieved.

python

```
tasks = Task.objects.only('title',
'due_date')  # Fetch only specific
fields
```

This reduces the amount of data returned, speeding up queries and reducing memory usage.

Optimizing React/Vue.js

Optimizing the frontend is equally important as optimizing the backend. Efficient frontend performance ensures a smooth user experience, particularly in **Single-Page Applications (SPAs)** like those built with **React** and **Vue.js**. In this section, we'll explore some performance optimization strategies for both React and Vue.js applications.

1. Optimizing React Performance

React is fast out of the box, but there are several ways to optimize React apps for performance as they grow larger and more complex.

Step 1: Code Splitting

Code splitting is a technique used to split your JavaScript bundle into smaller chunks, which are loaded only when needed. This reduces the initial load time and makes your app faster.

React provides a built-in method for code splitting through **React.lazy** and **Suspense**.

```javascript
import React, { Suspense, lazy }
from 'react';

const TaskList = lazy(() =>
import('./TaskList'));

function App() {
  return (
    <Suspense
fallback={<div>Loading...</div>}>
```

```
      <TaskList />
    </Suspense>
  );
}
```

Here, the TaskList component is only loaded when the user navigates to it, which reduces the initial bundle size.

Step 2: Memoization

Memoization helps to prevent unnecessary re-renders by caching the results of expensive function calls. In React, you can use **React.memo** to memoize components and **useMemo** to memoize values inside a component.

- **Memoizing a Component:**

javascript

```
const TaskItem = React.memo(({
task }) => {
  return <div>{task.title}</div>;
```

```javascript
});
```

This ensures that the component is only re-rendered if its props change.

- **Memoizing a Value:**

```javascript
const filteredTasks = useMemo(()
=> {
  return tasks.filter(task =>
task.completed);
}, [tasks]);
```

useMemo will only recompute filteredTasks if tasks changes, avoiding unnecessary recalculations.

Step 3: Virtualization

For applications displaying long lists of items, **virtualization** can improve performance by rendering only the visible items on the screen, instead of rendering the entire list. This technique can be implemented using libraries like **react-window** or **react-virtualized.**

```javascript
import { FixedSizeList as List }
from 'react-window';

function TaskList({ tasks }) {
  return (
    <List
      height={400}
      itemCount={tasks.length}
      itemSize={35}
      width={300}
    >
      {({ index, style }) => (
        <div
style={style}>{tasks[index].title}
</div>
      )}
    </List>
```

```
  );
}
```

This renders only the visible items in the list, dramatically improving performance.

---

2. Optimizing Vue.js Performance

Vue.js also offers several strategies for improving application performance. Here are some essential techniques.

Step 1: Lazy Loading with Vue Router

Like React's code splitting, Vue Router supports lazy loading of routes. This can significantly reduce the size of the initial bundle.

```javascript
const TaskList = () =>
import('./components/TaskList.vue'
);
```

```
const routes = [
  {
    path: '/tasks',
    component: TaskList,
  },
];
```

With this approach, the TaskList component will only be loaded when the user navigates to the /tasks route.

Step 2: Memoization with Vue.js

Vue's **computed properties** are automatically cached, meaning they are recalculated only when their dependencies change. This is a simple form of memoization and is useful for optimizing performance when dealing with complex data transformations.

```
javascript
```

```
computed: {
  filteredTasks() {
    return this.tasks.filter(task
=> task.completed);
  },
}
```

This ensures that the filteredTasks array is recalculated only when the tasks array changes, optimizing performance.

Step 3: Avoiding Unnecessary Re-renders

Vue.js automatically optimizes component updates, but there are cases where manual optimization is needed. You can use **v-once** to ensure that a component is rendered only once, and **v-show** to control visibility without re-rendering.

```vue
<div v-if="isVisible" v-once>
```

```
    This content will only render
once.
</div>
```

Step 4: Using Web Workers

For CPU-intensive tasks, **Web Workers** can help offload the processing to a background thread, ensuring that the main UI thread remains responsive. Vue can easily integrate with Web Workers to handle such tasks.

javascript

```javascript
const worker = new
Worker('worker.js');
worker.postMessage('start');
worker.onmessage = (event) => {
  console.log('Worker result:',
event.data);
};
```

This allows you to keep your application fast even when performing heavy computations.

Conclusion

In this chapter, we covered essential **performance optimization strategies** for both **Django** and **React/Vue.js**. By implementing caching, database indexing, and query optimization in Django, and optimizing React and Vue.js with techniques like lazy loading, code splitting, and memoization, you can significantly improve the performance of your full-stack application.

These strategies will help your application scale efficiently, providing a seamless user experience even as traffic increases. As your application grows, continue to monitor and fine-tune its performance to ensure that it meets the needs of your users.

Great work! You've now learned how to optimize both the backend and frontend of your full-stack application. Keep practicing and experimenting with these strategies to build faster, more scalable applications. **You've got this!**

Chapter 9: Building a Blog Application

In this chapter, we will guide you through creating a **full-stack blog application** using **Django** for the backend and **React** for the frontend. We will cover how to set up the blog's main features, including creating blog posts, managing user profiles, adding comment sections, and enabling post editing.

This project is ideal for those looking to understand how to combine Django and React to build a dynamic and interactive web application. By the end of this chapter, you will have a complete blog application with the following features:

- **User authentication** (sign up, login, and logout)

- **CRUD functionality** for blog posts (create, read, update, and delete)

- **Comment sections** for posts

- **User profiles** for managing personal information and posts

- **Post editing** capabilities

We'll break the project into clear, manageable steps so you can easily follow along and build your own blog application.

Setting Up the Backend: Django

Before we start building the React frontend, let's set up the backend with Django. The backend will handle user authentication, manage blog posts, and store comments.

1. Setting Up Django Project

Let's start by creating a new Django project.

Step 1: Install Django

If you haven't already installed Django, you can do so with the following command:

```bash

pip install Django
```

Step 2: Create a New Django Project

Create a new Django project by running:

bash

```
django-admin startproject
blog_project
cd blog_project
```

Step 3: Create a Django App

Next, we'll create a Django app for the blog functionality. Run the following command:

bash

```
python manage.py startapp blog
Now, add the blog app to your
INSTALLED_APPS in settings.py:
python

INSTALLED_APPS = [
    'django.contrib.admin',
```

```python
'django.contrib.auth',
'django.contrib.contenttypes',
'django.contrib.sessions',
'django.contrib.messages',
'django.contrib.staticfiles',
'blog',  # Add your app here
]
```

Step 4: Set Up Database Models

We'll create models to represent **BlogPost**, **Comment**, and **UserProfile** (a custom model for user-related data). Open blog/models.py and define the models:

python

```python
from django.db import models
from django.contrib.auth.models import User

class BlogPost(models.Model):
```

```python
    title =
models.CharField(max_length=255)
    content = models.TextField()
    author =
models.ForeignKey(User,
on_delete=models.CASCADE)
    created_at =
models.DateTimeField(auto_now_add=
True)
    updated_at =
models.DateTimeField(auto_now=True
)

    def __str__(self):
        return self.title


class Comment(models.Model):
    post =
models.ForeignKey(BlogPost,
related_name='comments',
on_delete=models.CASCADE)
```

```python
    author = models.CharField(max_length=100)
    content = models.TextField()
    created_at = models.DateTimeField(auto_now_add=True)

    def __str__(self):
        return f"Comment by {self.author}"

class UserProfile(models.Model):
    user = models.OneToOneField(User, on_delete=models.CASCADE)
    bio = models.TextField(blank=True)

    def __str__(self):
        return self.user.username
```

Step 5: Migrate the Database

Run the following commands to create the necessary database tables:

```bash
python manage.py makemigrations
python manage.py migrate
```

This will create the tables for BlogPost, Comment, and UserProfile in your database.

---

2. Setting Up Views and URLs

Now that we have our models, let's create views for handling the blog's functionality, such as displaying posts, adding comments, and editing posts.

Step 1: Create Views

In blog/views.py, create views to handle displaying posts, adding comments, and allowing post editing:

python

```python
from django.shortcuts import render, get_object_or_404, redirect
from .models import BlogPost, Comment
from .forms import BlogPostForm, CommentForm

def home(request):
    posts = BlogPost.objects.all()
    return render(request, 'home.html', {'posts': posts})

def post_detail(request, post_id):
```

```python
    post =
get_object_or_404(BlogPost,
id=post_id)
    comments = post.comments.all()
    if request.method == "POST":
        comment_form =
CommentForm(request.POST)
        if
comment_form.is_valid():
            comment =
comment_form.save(commit=False)
            comment.post = post
            comment.save()
            return
redirect('post_detail',
post_id=post.id)
    else:
        comment_form =
CommentForm()
    return render(request,
'post_detail.html', {'post': post,
```

```python
            'comments': comments,
            'comment_form': comment_form})


def create_post(request):
    if request.method == "POST":
        form = BlogPostForm(request.POST)
        if form.is_valid():
            form.save()
            return redirect('home')
    else:
        form = BlogPostForm()
    return render(request,
'create_post.html', {'form':
form})


def edit_post(request, post_id):
    post = get_object_or_404(BlogPost,
id=post_id)
```

```
    if request.method == "POST":
        form =
BlogPostForm(request.POST,
instance=post)
        if form.is_valid():
            form.save()
            return
redirect('post_detail',
post_id=post.id)
    else:
        form =
BlogPostForm(instance=post)
    return render(request,
'edit_post.html', {'form': form})
```

Step 2: Create URLs for Views

In blog/urls.py, set up URL patterns to link the views to URLs:

```python

from django.urls import path
```

```
from . import views

urlpatterns = [
    path('', views.home,
name='home'),
    path('post/<int:post_id>/',
views.post_detail,
name='post_detail'),
    path('create/',
views.create_post,
name='create_post'),
    path('edit/<int:post_id>/',
views.edit_post,
name='edit_post'),
]
```

Step 3: Create Templates

Create the following templates to display posts, comments, and forms for creating and editing posts:

- home.html: Displays all posts

- post_detail.html: Displays a single post and its comments

- create_post.html: Form for creating a new post

- edit_post.html: Form for editing an existing post

Example home.html:

```html

{% for post in posts %}
    <h2><a href="{% url
'post_detail' post.id %}">{{
post.title }}</a></h2>
    <p>{{
post.content|truncatewords:30
}}</p>
{% endfor %}
```

Building the Frontend: React

Now that the backend is set up, let's move to the frontend. In this section, we will build a React application that fetches and displays blog posts, allows users to comment on posts, and provides a user interface for post editing.

1. Setting Up React

Step 1: Create a React App

Create a new React application using **Create React App:**

```bash
bash
```

```bash
npx create-react-app blog-frontend
cd blog-frontend
```

Step 2: Install Axios for API Requests

To communicate with the Django backend, we'll use **Axios** for making HTTP requests. Install Axios:

```bash
bash
```

```bash
npm install axios
```

---

2. Displaying Blog Posts

Step 1: Create a PostList Component

In src/components/PostList.js, create a component that fetches and displays blog posts from Django's API:

```javascript
javascript
```

```
import React, { useState,
useEffect } from 'react';
import axios from 'axios';

const PostList = () => {
  const [posts, setPosts] =
useState([]);

  useEffect(() => {

axios.get('http://127.0.0.1:8000/a
pi/posts/')
      .then(response =>
setPosts(response.data))
      .catch(error =>
console.log(error));
  }, []);

  return (
    <div>
```

[227]

```
    <h1>Blog Posts</h1>
    <ul>
      {posts.map(post => (
        <li key={post.id}>
          <a
href={`/posts/${post.id}`}>{post.t
itle}</a>
        </li>
      ))}
    </ul>
  </div>
  );
};


export default PostList;
```

Step 2: Create Post Detail Component

Now, let's create a PostDetail component to display a single post along with its comments:

```javascript
```

```
import React, { useState,
useEffect } from 'react';
import axios from 'axios';

const PostDetail = ({ match }) =>
{
  const [post, setPost] =
useState(null);
  const [comments, setComments] =
useState([]);
  const [comment, setComment] =
useState('');

  useEffect(() => {
    const postId =
match.params.id;

axios.get(`http://127.0.0.1:8000/a
pi/posts/${postId}/`)
      .then(response =>
setPost(response.data));
```

```
axios.get(`http://127.0.0.1:8000/a
pi/posts/${postId}/comments/`)
        .then(response =>
setComments(response.data));
    }, [match.params.id]);


    const handleCommentSubmit = (e)
=> {
        e.preventDefault();
        const postId =
match.params.id;


axios.post(`http://127.0.0.1:8000/
api/posts/${postId}/comments/`, {
content: comment })
        .then(response =>
setComments([...comments,
response.data]));
        setComment('');
    };
```

```
if (!post) return
<p>Loading...</p>;

return (
  <div>
    <h1>{post.title}</h1>
    <p>{post.content}</p>
    <h2>Comments</h2>
    <ul>
      {comments.map(comment => (
        <li
key={comment.id}>{comment.content}
</li>
      ))}
    </ul>
    <form
onSubmit={handleCommentSubmit}>
      <textarea
        value={comment}
```

```
        onChange={ (e) =>
setComment(e.target.value)}
        placeholder="Add a
comment"
        />
        <button type="submit">Post
Comment</button>
      </form>
    </div>
  );
};


export default PostDetail;
```

---

3. Adding Post Editing

Step 1: Create an EditPost Component

In src/components/EditPost.js, create a form for editing blog posts:

javascript

```
import React, { useState,
useEffect } from 'react';
import axios from 'axios';

const EditPost = ({ match, history
}) => {
  const [title, setTitle] =
useState('');
  const [content, setContent] =
useState('');

  useEffect(() => {
    const postId =
match.params.id;

axios.get(`http://127.0.0.1:8000/a
pi/posts/${postId}/`)
      .then(response => {

setTitle(response.data.title);
```

```
setContent(response.data.content);
    });
}, [match.params.id]);

const handleSubmit = (e) => {
  e.preventDefault();
  const postId =
match.params.id;

axios.put(`http://127.0.0.1:8000/a
pi/posts/${postId}/`, { title,
content })
    .then(() =>
history.push(`/posts/${postId}`));
};

return (
  <div>
    <h1>Edit Post</h1>
```

```
        <form
onSubmit={handleSubmit}>
        <input
            type="text"
            value={title}
            onChange={(e) =>
setTitle(e.target.value)}
            placeholder="Title"
        />
        <textarea
            value={content}
            onChange={(e) =>
setContent(e.target.value)}
            placeholder="Content"
        />
        <button
type="submit">Update Post</button>
        </form>
    </div>
  );
};
```

```
export default EditPost;
```

Conclusion

In this chapter, you've learned how to build a full-stack **blog application** using **Django** for the backend and **React** for the frontend. We covered:

- **User authentication** using Django's built-in tools.

- **CRUD functionality** for managing blog posts, comments, and user profiles.

- **Creating and editing blog posts** with a React frontend.

- **Comment sections** for posts.

This blog app provides a solid foundation for understanding how to create full-stack applications using Django and React. With these skills, you can now build more complex features and expand your project further!

Great job! You've built a powerful, interactive blog application—keep experimenting and refining your skills. **You've got this!**

Chapter 10: Building an E-Commerce Application

In this chapter, we will guide you through the process of creating a **full-stack e-commerce application** using **Django** for the backend and **React** or **Vue.js** for the frontend. This application will include features such as product listings, cart functionality, and payment gateway integration.

Building an e-commerce site requires understanding how to manage users, products, and orders efficiently. We'll cover everything from product management to handling a shopping cart, and finally, integrating a **payment gateway** to accept payments.

By the end of this chapter, you will be able to:

- Create product listings with Django models and display them on the frontend.

- Implement shopping cart functionality with React/Vue.js.

- Integrate a payment gateway for accepting payments (we will use **Stripe** as an example).

Let's dive in!

Setting Up the Backend: Django

Before building the frontend, let's set up the **Django backend** to handle products, shopping carts, and orders.

1. Setting Up Django Project

Step 1: Install Django

First, ensure you have **Django** installed. If you don't have it yet, run:

bash

pip install django

Step 2: Create a New Django Project

Let's create a new Django project and app to handle our e-commerce features:

```bash
django-admin startproject
ecommerce_project
cd ecommerce_project
python manage.py startapp shop
```

Step 3: Configure the Django Settings

Add your shop app to INSTALLED_APPS in settings.py:

```python
INSTALLED_APPS = [
    'django.contrib.admin',
    'django.contrib.auth',
    'django.contrib.contenttypes',
    'django.contrib.sessions',
    'django.contrib.messages',
    'django.contrib.staticfiles',
    'shop',  # Your app here
]
```

You also need to configure your static files and media settings for product images:

python

```
MEDIA_URL = '/media/'
MEDIA_ROOT =
os.path.join(BASE_DIR, 'media')
```

Now, let's move on to creating the **models** for products and orders.

---

2. Creating Models for Products and Orders

Step 1: Product Model

Open shop/models.py and create a model for products:

python

```
from django.db import models
```

```python
class Product(models.Model):
    title =
models.CharField(max_length=100)
    description =
models.TextField()
    price =
models.DecimalField(max_digits=10,
decimal_places=2)
    image =
models.ImageField(upload_to='produ
cts/', null=True, blank=True)
    stock =
models.PositiveIntegerField()

    def __str__(self):
        return self.title
```

Step 2: Cart and Order Models

Now let's create models for the shopping cart and order functionality.

```python
python

class Cart(models.Model):
    user = models.ForeignKey('auth.User',
on_delete=models.CASCADE,
related_name='carts')
    created_at = models.DateTimeField(auto_now_add=True)


class CartItem(models.Model):
    cart = models.ForeignKey(Cart,
related_name='items',
on_delete=models.CASCADE)
    product = models.ForeignKey(Product,
on_delete=models.CASCADE)
    quantity = models.PositiveIntegerField()
```

```python
class Order(models.Model):
    user =
models.ForeignKey('auth.User',
on_delete=models.CASCADE,
related_name='orders')
    total_price =
models.DecimalField(max_digits=10,
decimal_places=2)
    created_at =
models.DateTimeField(auto_now_add=
True)
    status =
models.CharField(max_length=100,
default='Pending')
```

The Cart model will store the current shopping cart for a user, while the CartItem model stores the individual products in the cart. The Order model will track orders once a user completes the checkout process.

Step 3: Create Migrations

Run the following commands to create and apply migrations for these models:

bash

```
python manage.py makemigrations
python manage.py migrate
```

---

3. Setting Up Product and Cart Views

Now that we've created our models, let's set up views to interact with the database and render product listings, cart contents, and orders.

Step 1: Displaying Products

Create a view to display all products. In shop/views.py, add the following:

python

```python
from django.shortcuts import
render
from .models import Product

def product_list(request):
    products =
Product.objects.all()
    return render(request,
'shop/product_list.html',
{'products': products})
```

In the corresponding template product_list.html, you can display the list of products:

html

```html
{% for product in products %}
  <div>
    <h3>{{ product.title }}</h3>
    <p>{{ product.description
}}</p>
    <p>${{ product.price }}</p>
```

```
<img src="{{ product.image.url
}}" alt="{{ product.title }}">
    <button>Add to Cart</button>
  </div>
{% endfor %}
```

Step 2: Handling the Cart

Let's set up a basic view to display the cart items.
In views.py, add:

```python
from .models import Cart, CartItem

def cart_detail(request):
    cart =
Cart.objects.get(user=request.user
)
    items =
CartItem.objects.filter(cart=cart)
```

```
    return render(request,
'shop/cart_detail.html', {'items':
items})
```

In the cart_detail.html template:
html

```
{% for item in items %}
  <div>
    <h4>{{ item.product.title
}}</h4>
    <p>Quantity: {{ item.quantity
}}</p>
    <p>Total: ${{
item.product.price * item.quantity
}}</p>
  </div>
{% endfor %}
```

Step 3: Order Handling

Create a view to place an order once the user checks out. For simplicity, we'll assume that payment is processed separately, and the order is only placed once the cart is finalized.

python

```python
from django.shortcuts import redirect
from .models import Order

def place_order(request):
    cart = Cart.objects.get(user=request.user)
    total_price = sum(item.product.price * item.quantity for item in cart.items.all())
    order = Order.objects.create(user=request.user, total_price=total_price)
```

```
    cart.items.all().delete()    #
Clear the cart after order
placement
    return
redirect('order_detail',
order_id=order.id)
```

---

4. Handling Payments with Stripe

To accept payments, we'll integrate **Stripe** into our Django app. First, install the **Stripe** library:

bash

```
pip install stripe
```

Step 1: Setting Up Stripe

Go to the Stripe website to create a Stripe account and obtain your **API keys**. Add these keys to your settings.py:

python

```
STRIPE_TEST_SECRET_KEY = 'your-
secret-key'
STRIPE_TEST_PUBLIC_KEY = 'your-
public-key'
```

Step 2: Create Stripe Payment View

In your views, set up a payment view that integrates with Stripe:

```python
python

import stripe
from django.conf import settings
from django.shortcuts import render

stripe.api_key = settings.STRIPE_TEST_SECRET_KEY

def create_checkout_session(request):
```

```python
checkout_session =
stripe.checkout.Session.create(

payment_method_types=['card'],
        line_items=[
            {
                'price_data': {
                    'currency':
'usd',

'product_data': {
                        'name':
'Product Name',
                },
                'unit_amount':
2000,
                },
                'quantity': 1,
            },
        ],
        mode='payment',
```

```
success_url=request.build_absolute
_uri('/success/'),

cancel_url=request.build_absolute_
uri('/cancel/'),
    )
    return
redirect(checkout_session.url)
```

In your frontend, create a button to initiate the checkout process.

Building the Frontend: React or Vue.js

Now that we have our Django backend set up, it's time to build the frontend using **React** or **Vue.js**.

1. Setting Up React

Let's start by creating a **React frontend** to interact with the Django backend.

Step 1: Install React

Create a new React project:

```bash
```

```
npx create-react-app ecommerce-
frontend
cd ecommerce-frontend
```

```
npm start
```

Step 2: Fetching Product Data

In src/App.js, fetch the products from the Django backend and display them:

```javascript
import React, { useEffect,
useState } from 'react';
import axios from 'axios';

const App = () => {
  const [products, setProducts] =
useState([]);

  useEffect(() => {

axios.get('http://127.0.0.1:8000/a
pi/products/')
      .then(response =>
setProducts(response.data))
```

```
      .catch(error =>
console.log(error));
  }, []);


  return (
    <div>
      <h1>Product List</h1>
      <ul>
        {products.map(product => (
          <li key={product.id}>

<h2>{product.title}</h2>

<p>{product.description}</p>

<p>${product.price}</p>
            <button>Add to
Cart</button>
          </li>
        ))}
      </ul>
```

```
    </div>
  );
}
```

```
export default App;
```

Step 3: Cart Functionality

For cart functionality, you can store cart items in **React's state** or **localStorage**. Use **context** or **Redux** to manage global state for the cart.

---

2. Setting Up Vue.js

Alternatively, if you prefer using **Vue.js** instead of React, follow these steps.

Step 1: Install Vue.js

You can create a Vue.js project using Vue CLI:

```bash
```

```
npm install -g @vue/cli
```

```
vue create ecommerce-frontend
cd ecommerce-frontend
npm run serve
```

Step 2: Fetch Products with Vue.js

In src/App.vue, fetch the products and display them:

```vue
vue

<template>
  <div>
    <h1>Product List</h1>
    <ul>
      <li v-for="product in
products" :key="product.id">
        <h2>{{ product.title
}}</h2>
        <p>{{ product.description
}}</p>
        <p>${{ product.price
}}</p>
```

```
    <button
@click="addToCart(product)">Add to
Cart</button>
      </li>
    </ul>
  </div>
</template>

<script>
import axios from 'axios';

export default {
  data() {
    return {
      products: [],
    };
  },
  mounted() {

axios.get('http://127.0.0.1:8000/a
pi/products/')
```

```
    .then(response => {
        this.products =
response.data;
    })
    .catch(error =>
console.log(error));
  },
  methods: {
    addToCart(product) {
      // Handle add to cart logic
    }
  }
};
</script>
```

Conclusion

In this chapter, we've walked through building a **full-stack e-commerce application** using **Django** for the backend and **React** or **Vue.js** for the frontend. We've covered:

- **Setting up models** for products, cart items, and orders in Django.

- **Creating product listings**, handling **cart functionality**, and setting up **order management**.

- Integrating **Stripe** to handle payments.

- Building the **React** or **Vue.js frontend** to interact with the backend.

With these techniques, you now have a solid foundation for building dynamic, fully-featured e-commerce applications. From here, you can further enhance the app by adding features like **user authentication**, **product categories**, **search functionality**, and more. Keep experimenting, and continue building your skills! **You've got this!**

Conclusion: Next Steps in Full-Stack Development

As we've explored throughout this book, full-stack development is an exciting and powerful way to build modern, dynamic applications. Whether you're creating a blog, an e-commerce site, or a complex enterprise-level app, full-stack development empowers you to design, develop, and deploy both the backend and frontend of an application.

But as you continue to grow as a full-stack developer, you'll inevitably encounter the challenges of scaling your application, improving performance, and maintaining it efficiently. This final chapter will guide you through these critical aspects of full-stack development and help you take the next steps in your learning journey.

In this chapter, we'll explore two main areas:

1. **Scaling Your Application** – How to scale your full-stack applications to handle more traffic, users, and data.

2. **Learning Resources and Continuing Education** – How to continue improving your skills and staying up to date with the latest trends in full-stack development.

Let's get started!

Scaling Your Application

As your application grows, you'll need to consider how to scale it effectively. Scaling refers to the process of making sure your application can handle an increasing number of users, requests, and data without slowing down or crashing. There are several techniques and architectural decisions that can help you achieve this, from **load balancing** to implementing **microservices**.

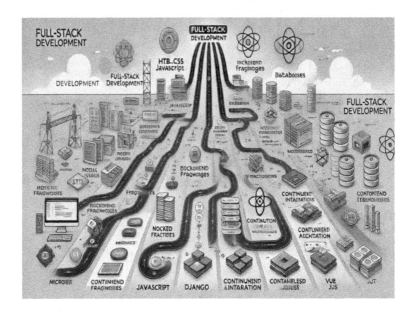

Let's break down some of the most important concepts for scaling your full-stack applications:

---

1. Load Balancing

One of the first strategies for scaling an application is **load balancing**. Load balancing is the process of distributing incoming traffic across multiple servers or instances to ensure that no single server is overwhelmed. This is particularly useful when your application experiences a surge in traffic.

How Load Balancing Works

Imagine your web application is like a restaurant. The customers (requests) come in, and the servers (web servers) are responsible for serving them. If one server is overwhelmed with too many requests, it can't serve new customers quickly. Instead, the restaurant uses multiple servers to handle customers more efficiently. This is essentially what a load balancer does.

A **load balancer** sits between the client (user) and your servers, distributing incoming requests based on various algorithms like **round-robin, least connections**, or **IP hash**.

- **Round-robin**: Distributes requests evenly across servers.

- **Least connections**: Sends requests to the server with the least number of active connections.

- **IP hash**: Routes requests from the same client (IP) to the same server, ensuring session consistency.

Real-World Example:

Consider **AWS Elastic Load Balancing (ELB)** or **NGINX** as load balancing tools. With AWS ELB, traffic can be automatically distributed to EC2 instances. NGINX can be used as a reverse proxy to route requests between multiple backend services.

Why Load Balancing is Important:

- **High Availability**: If one server goes down, the load balancer can route traffic to healthy servers, keeping the application running.

- **Efficient Resource Usage**: Ensures no single server becomes a bottleneck by distributing traffic.

- **Fault Tolerance**: Helps your app stay online even when individual servers fail.

---

2. Horizontal Scaling

Horizontal scaling, also known as **scaling out**, involves adding more servers to your application infrastructure. This is in contrast to **vertical scaling**, where you upgrade a single server by adding more CPU, RAM, or storage.

How Horizontal Scaling Works

With horizontal scaling, you add more machines or instances to handle additional load. For instance, if one server can only handle 1000 requests per second, adding another server allows your application to handle 2000 requests per second. This scaling strategy is ideal for handling high traffic and large data volumes.

Example in Practice:

In a Django application, you might have multiple instances running behind a load balancer. For your React frontend, multiple web servers or containers can serve the app, with each instance running on a different machine. Using cloud services like AWS, **Google Cloud**, or **Azure**, you can scale your infrastructure with ease by spinning up more server instances based on demand.

Why Horizontal Scaling is Important:

- **Cost-Effective**: It's often cheaper to add more low-cost machines than to upgrade one high-powered server.

- **Flexibility**: You can scale out or scale in dynamically depending on your application's needs.

- **Fault Tolerance**: If one server goes down, others can still handle the traffic.

---

3. Vertical Scaling

While horizontal scaling involves adding more servers, **vertical scaling** focuses on upgrading your existing server. This can include adding more CPU power, RAM, or storage to a single instance.

When to Use Vertical Scaling:

Vertical scaling is often easier and quicker to implement than horizontal scaling, but it has limits. It's suitable when you need to improve the performance of a single server or when your application is small to medium-sized and doesn't require extensive scaling.

Why Vertical Scaling is Important:

- **Simple to Implement**: Upgrading an existing server is straightforward compared to setting up multiple servers.

- **For Small Applications**: Ideal for small applications that do not require many distributed components.

Drawback of Vertical Scaling:

- **Limits to Expansion**: Eventually, you will reach the hardware limits of your server. This is why horizontal scaling is often preferred for larger applications.

4. Microservices Architecture

As applications grow in complexity, **microservices** architecture can be a great way to scale your application. Instead of building a monolithic application (where all components are tightly coupled and reside in a single server or process), microservices break down the application into smaller, independent services.

What Are Microservices?

In a microservices architecture, each service is self-contained and performs a specific business function. For example, in an e-commerce app:

- **Product Service**: Handles product management (creating, updating, deleting products).

- **Order Service**: Manages user orders.

- **Cart Service**: Manages the shopping cart.

- **Payment Service**: Handles payment processing.

Each service communicates with others through APIs, making them independent and scalable.

Benefits of Microservices:

- **Scalability**: Each service can be scaled independently. For instance, if the **Payment Service** experiences high load during a sale, you can scale that service alone.

- **Maintainability**: Smaller services are easier to maintain and deploy independently.

- **Flexibility**: Microservices allow you to use different technologies for different services. For example, you might use Django for the **Order Service** and Node.js for the **Payment Service**.

Challenges of Microservices:

- **Complexity**: Managing multiple services requires tools like Docker, Kubernetes, and service discovery.

- **Inter-service Communication**: You need a robust method for services to communicate, such as using **REST APIs** or **gRPC**.

Learning Resources and Continuing Education

As you continue on your journey as a full-stack developer, it's essential to keep learning and staying updated on the latest technologies, best practices, and frameworks. Below, I've compiled a list of **recommended resources** that will help you expand your skills and stay ahead of the curve.

1. Books to Deepen Your Knowledge

- **"Two Scoops of Django" by Audrey Roy Greenfeld & Daniel Roy Greenfeld**: This book provides best practices and tips for writing clean, scalable Django code. It's perfect for intermediate to advanced Django developers.

- **"Eloquent JavaScript" by Marijn Haverbeke**: A great book to dive deep into JavaScript and understand its quirks and features. It's useful for both React and Vue.js developers.

- **"Learning React" by Alex Banks and Eve Porcello**: A hands-on guide to building real-world React applications, this book will help you become proficient in React development.

- **"Vue.js Up and Running" by Callum Macrae:** This book is a fantastic introduction to Vue.js, offering practical examples and covering important concepts for building modern web applications with Vue.

- **"Designing Data-Intensive Applications" by Martin Kleppmann:** This book covers the architecture and tools for building scalable, high-performance applications that handle large amounts of data.

---

2. Online Courses

- Udemy:

  - **Complete Guide to Django:** A comprehensive course for learning Django, including how to build, deploy, and scale full-stack applications.

- **Modern React with Redux**: A highly rated course for learning React, Redux, and building full-fledged applications.

- **Coursera:**

  - **Full-Stack Web Development with React Specialization** (offered by The Hong Kong University of Science and Technology): This course covers both front-end and back-end development, focusing on React and Node.js.

- **Pluralsight:**

  - **Full Stack Web Development with Angular and Django**: A great course for those interested in using Angular for the frontend alongside Django in the backend.

---

3. Blogs and Online Communities

- **Stack Overflow**: The go-to platform for solving programming problems and discussing development topics. Join the **Django**, **React**, and **Vue.js** communities to ask questions and learn from others.

- **Dev.to**: A platform where developers share blog posts, tutorials, and experiences. Look for tags like **#Django**, **#ReactJS**, **#VueJS**, and **#FullStackDevelopment** for relevant articles.

- **Reddit**:

  - **r/django**: A subreddit dedicated to Django, where you can ask questions, share your projects, and learn from other developers.

- r/reactjs: The go-to community for all things React.

- r/vuejs: If you're interested in Vue.js, this subreddit has a vibrant community of Vue developers.

- **Medium**: Many full-stack developers and companies share in-depth articles on Medium. Search for tags like **Full Stack Development, Django, React,** and **Vue** to stay up to date with the latest trends and practices.

4. Developer Conferences and Meetups

- **DjangoCon**: An annual conference dedicated to Django developers, with talks ranging from beginner to advanced topics.

- **ReactConf**: The official React conference, where you can hear about the latest advancements in React and learn from the experts.

- **VueConf**: The official conference for Vue.js, where you can meet the Vue community and learn best practices.

- **Local Meetups**: Check out platforms like **Meetup.com** to find local development groups and events related to Django, React, or Vue.js.

Conclusion

Full-stack development is a powerful skill that can open doors to many exciting opportunities. From building small projects to scaling massive applications, the knowledge you've gained in this book will serve as a solid foundation for your journey. As you continue to grow, remember that learning is a never-ending process. The tech industry is constantly evolving, and staying updated with the latest trends and best practices is essential.

Whether you're scaling your applications using advanced techniques like **load balancing, horizontal scaling,** and **microservices,** or continuing your education with books, courses, and communities, the future of full-stack development is bright. You now have the tools, resources, and mindset to build amazing applications and solve complex problems.

Keep building, keep learning, and most importantly, **keep having fun with full-stack development. You've got this!**

Appendices

Appendix A: Common Errors and Troubleshooting

In this appendix, we will guide you through some of the **common errors** developers face when working with **Django**, **React**, and **Vue.js**, and provide practical advice for troubleshooting these issues. Whether you're building a simple app or a complex full-stack project, encountering errors is part of the development process. Understanding how to approach and resolve these errors will make you a more effective developer.

We'll break down the errors and troubleshooting steps into the following sections:

1. **Django Errors**

2. **React Errors**

3. **Vue.js Errors**

---

1. Django Errors

Django is a powerful backend framework, but it's not uncommon to run into errors while building applications. Below are some common errors and how to fix them.

Error: "ModuleNotFoundError: No module named 'django'"

This error occurs when Django is not installed in your Python environment. To resolve this, ensure you have installed Django in the correct environment. You can install Django using the following command:

```bash

pip install django
```

If you're using a virtual environment, ensure that the environment is activated before installing Django.

Error: "DatabaseError: no such table: ..."

This error typically occurs when Django is trying to query a table that doesn't exist in the database. It can happen after creating new models or making migrations. The solution is to run the migrations to create the necessary tables in your database:

bash

```
python manage.py makemigrations
python manage.py migrate
```

Error: "ModuleNotFoundError: No module named 'django.contrib.sites'"

If you are using django-allauth for authentication and see this error, it means that the

django.contrib.sites module is missing in your INSTALLED_APPS setting. To fix it, add 'django.contrib.sites' to your INSTALLED_APPS in settings.py:

python

```
INSTALLED_APPS = [
    'django.contrib.sites',
    # other apps
]
```

Error: "ImportError: cannot import name '...' from 'django.urls' ..."

This error typically occurs when you're using the wrong import path for views or URL patterns. Make sure you're importing views or functions correctly based on the version of Django you're using.

For example, in Django 2.x, URL handling changed slightly, and you need to use path() instead of url(). If you have:

python

```
from django.conf.urls import url
# This is old!
```

You should replace it with:

python

```
from django.urls import path  #
This is the correct import for
Django 2.x+
```

Error: "ValueError: The 'django.contrib.staticfiles' app is required to use staticfiles."

This error is usually caused when the static files app is missing or misconfigured in your project.

To fix it, ensure that 'django.contrib.staticfiles' is added to INSTALLED_APPS in settings.py.

python

```python
INSTALLED_APPS = [
    'django.contrib.staticfiles',
# Ensure this line is included
    # other apps
]
```

---

2. React Errors

React is a widely-used frontend library, and while it's known for its efficiency, developers frequently encounter errors. Below are common issues in React and how to troubleshoot them.

Error: "Module not found: Can't resolve 'react'"

This error occurs when React is not properly installed. To resolve this, make sure that React is installed in your project's node_modules folder. Run the following commands to ensure React is installed:

```bash
```

```bash
npm install react react-dom
```

If you're using yarn, you can install React with:

```bash
```

```bash
yarn add react react-dom
```

Error: "Uncaught TypeError: Cannot read property 'map' of undefined"

This error occurs when you try to call .map() on an array that is undefined or null. To fix this, ensure that the variable you're trying to map over is initialized as an array or has data before you try to map it.

For example:

```javascript

const [posts, setPosts] =
useState([]);

useEffect(() => {
  axios.get('api/posts')
    .then(response =>
setPosts(response.data))
    .catch(error =>
console.log(error));
}, []);

return (
  <div>
    {posts && posts.length > 0 ? (
      posts.map(post => <div
key={post.id}>{post.title}</div>)
    ) : (
      <p>Loading...</p>
    )}
```

```
    </div>
);
```

Here, we're ensuring posts is an array before using .map().

Error: "Warning: Each child in a list should have a unique 'key' prop."

React requires each element in a list to have a unique key prop to optimize rendering. You might encounter this warning if you render a list of elements without providing a key.

To resolve this, ensure that every item in the list has a unique key attribute:

```javascript

return (
  <ul>
    {posts.map((post) => (
      <li
key={post.id}>{post.title}</li>
```

```
  ) ) }
 </ul>
);
```

Error: "Error: Too many re-renders. React limits the number of renders to prevent an infinite loop."

This error occurs when a component re-renders continuously. It often happens due to improper state changes or setting state inside the render method. Make sure state updates are done inside appropriate lifecycle methods or hooks like useEffect().

javascript

```
useEffect(() => {
  setPosts(fetchPosts());
}, []); // Adding empty dependency
array to avoid infinite loop
```

3. Vue.js Errors

Vue.js is another popular JavaScript framework that's known for its simplicity. However, as with any framework, errors can still occur. Below are common errors encountered in Vue.js applications.

Error: "Module not found: Error: Can't resolve 'vue'"

This error occurs when Vue is not installed in your project. To fix this, ensure that Vue is installed:

```bash
```

```bash
npm install vue
```

If you're using yarn, run:

```bash
```

```bash
yarn add vue
```

Error: "Cannot read property 'xxx' of undefined"

This error often occurs when trying to access a property of an object that hasn't been initialized yet. To fix this, ensure that the object exists before trying to access its properties.

For example, if you're accessing a property inside data:

```javascript
data() {
  return {
    post: null,
  };
},
mounted() {

axios.get('/api/post').then(respon
se => {
    this.post = response.data;
```

```
   });
},
```

Before using the post object, check if it's defined:

```html
html
```

```
<div v-if="post">
  <h1>{{ post.title }}</h1>
</div>
```

Error: "Vue.js Warning: You are using the runtime-only build of Vue where the template compiler is not available."

This error happens if you're using the **runtime-only build** of Vue and trying to compile templates on the client-side. To fix this, ensure that you're using the **runtime+compiler** version of Vue.

In your webpack.config.js, make sure you're including the correct version:

javascript

```
module.exports = {

  resolve: {

    alias: {

      vue$: 'vue/dist/vue.esm.js',

    },

  },

};
```

Error: "Property or method 'xxx' is not defined on the instance but referenced during render."

This error occurs when you reference a property in your template that does not exist in the data, computed, or methods sections of the Vue instance. Ensure that the property is defined before using it in the template.

For example, ensure message exists:

nomnullgetName
mlrawrawraw

javascript

```
data() {
  return {
    message: 'Hello, Vue!',
  };
}
```

Appendix B: Recommended Tools and Libraries

To enhance your development workflow and improve the performance of your Django, React, and Vue.js applications, here's a list of essential tools and libraries that you should be familiar with.

1. Django Tools and Libraries

Django Rest Framework (DRF)

For building RESTful APIs, the **Django Rest Framework** (DRF) is an essential tool. It provides easy serialization, authentication, and view management for APIs.

Install it with:

```bash
```

```
pip install djangorestframework
```

Celery

For handling asynchronous tasks like sending emails or processing payments in the background, **Celery** is a great choice. It integrates seamlessly with Django.

Install it with:

```bash
```

```
pip install celery
```

django-allauth

For user authentication, registration, and social authentication (Google, Facebook, etc.), **django-allauth** is a powerful tool that can simplify your authentication process.

Install it with:

```
bash
```

```
pip install django-allauth
```

django-extensions

django-extensions provides useful management commands like shell_plus, show_urls, and others that can make your development process smoother.

Install it with:

```
bash
```

```
pip install django-extensions
```

---

2. React Tools and Libraries

Axios

Axios is a promise-based HTTP client that works in both browsers and Node.js. It's widely used for making API requests.

Install it with:

```bash
```

```
npm install axios
```

React Router

For handling navigation and routing in React, **React Router** is a must-have library. It allows you to manage navigation between different components/pages.

Install it with:

```bash
bash
```

```bash
npm install react-router-dom
```

Redux

For state management in larger React applications, **Redux** is a powerful library. It helps you manage global state in a predictable way.

Install it with:

```bash
bash
```

```bash
npm install redux react-redux
```

React Query

For managing and caching server state in React, **React Query** is a great tool. It simplifies data fetching, caching, and synchronization with the backend.

Install it with:

```bash
bash
```

```
npm install react-query
```

---

3. Vue.js Tools and Libraries

Vuex

For state management in Vue.js, **Vuex** is a popular library. It centralizes the state management across all components in a Vue application.

Install it with:

bash

```
npm install vuex
```

Vue Router

For handling routing in Vue.js, **Vue Router** allows you to manage different views or pages in your application.

Install it with:

```bash
```

```bash
npm install vue-router
```

Vuetify

If you want to build beautiful, responsive user interfaces, **Vuetify** is a material design component library for Vue.js that makes it easy to create professional-looking apps.

Install it with:

```bash
```

```bash
npm install vuetify
```

Vue CLI

To quickly scaffold new Vue projects, **Vue CLI** is a powerful tool that sets up a project with build configurations and plugin support.

Install it with:

```bash
```

```
npm install -g @vue/cli
```

Conclusion

In this appendix, we covered some of the most common errors you might face when developing with Django, React, and Vue.js, and we provided practical troubleshooting steps. Additionally, we introduced a list of essential tools and libraries that can significantly enhance your development workflow and make your applications more powerful.

By equipping yourself with these resources and troubleshooting strategies, you will be better prepared to tackle any challenges that arise during your full-stack development journey. Happy coding, and keep pushing forward—you've got this!

www.ingramcontent.com/pod-product-compliance
Lightning Source LLC
LaVergne TN
LVHW051434050326
832903LV00030BD/3073